Can you really have it all?

Nicola Horlick was educated at Cheltenham Ladies' College, Birkenhead High School GPDST and Balliol College, Oxford, where she gained a degree in Jurisprudence. In 1983, she joined S G Warburg, the merchant bank, as a graduate trainee and was appointed a director in 1989. In 1991, she moved to Morgan Grenfell where she was in charge of the UK pension fund business. She now works for Société Générale, the French bank. Nicola is married to Tim, an investment banker, and has five children.

Nicola Horlick

Can you really have it all?

PAN BOOKS

First published 1997 by Macmillan

This edition published 1998 by Pan Books
an imprint of Macmillan Publishers Ltd
25 Eccleston Place, London SW1W 9NF
and Basingstoke

Associated companies throughout the world

ISBN 0 330 35459 0

1 3 5 7 9 8 6 4 2

A CIP catalogue record for this book is available from
the British Library.

Typeset by SetSystems Ltd, Saffron Walden, Essex
Printed and bound in Great Britain by
Mackays of Chatham plc, Chatham, Kent

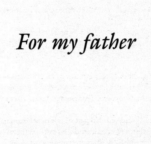

For my father

ACKNOWLEDGEMENTS

I would like to thank my editor, Allegra Huston, for the enormous amount of work that she has put into this book. She ended up spending much more time on it than she had originally anticipated and it was, no doubt, difficult dealing with someone who is more used to numbers than words. I would also like to thank Clare Alexander of Macmillan for believing that I could write this book and choosing Allegra to help me. Thanks must also go to my agent, Abner Stein. Most of all, I would like to thank my husband Tim. He has had to spend endless evenings on his own whilst I have sat at the computer. His support over the last few months has allowed me to cope.

I owe a great deal to the doctors and nurses at Great Ormond Street Hospital. Without them, we so easily could have lost our child. In recognition of what they have done, I have asked for the proceeds from the sale of this book to go to the REACH Fund at Great Ormond Street Hospital.

Finally, I would like to thank all the members of the public who have stopped me in the street and wished me well over the last few months. Knowing that I had your support was a great comfort to me.

one

Christmas is my favourite time of year. I love the smell of pine which fills the room when you first put up the Christmas tree. I love going to carol concerts and watching the children singing song after song and remembering every word. I love planning what I am going to give everyone for Christmas and watching the expressions of excitement on the children's faces as they unwrap their presents.

For any mother, Christmas is a busy time of year, but for a working mother, it is exceptionally so. As well as going to work every day, you have to find time to buy all the presents, wrap them, make the Christmas cake and pudding and go to the school carol concert. The more children you have, the greater the burden. There are more presents to wrap and possibly more than one carol concert to go to. I love Christmas, but by the time it is over, I am absolutely exhausted and go back to work for a rest.

Christmas 1996 was particularly busy. I had a six-month-old baby and four other children, one of whom was sick and had recently been in hospital. I also had a responsible job. I was Managing Director of Morgan Grenfell Investment Management, the subsidiary of Morgan Grenfell Asset Management which was responsible for managing money for UK pension funds and private clients. Most major companies in Britain have pension funds which are there to ensure that employees are provided for when they retire. In some cases, only the employer contributes, in others the employer and the employee contribute. There is always a board of trustees to watch over the assets and make sure that they are being properly managed. There are a number of large fund management houses in the UK, most of which emanated from the British merchant banks. The fund manager is responsible for investing the money in stocks and shares in the UK and overseas.

I had joined Morgan Grenfell in 1991 from Mercury Asset Management (the largest British-owned asset management company) and had found a business which was in decline. The performance of the funds which Morgan Grenfell managed had been inferior to that achieved by other leading fund managers and, as a result, clients were leaving. My brief was to turn the business round.

By the middle of 1996, I was proud to be in charge of a business that had grown fivefold in terms of the amount of money it managed on behalf of its clients and had the best performance figures amongst the major houses in London over one, three and five years. It had been the result of five years of hard work by me and my team. Some of them had been at Morgan Grenfell when I arrived and others I had recruited from outside. Acknowledgement of our success had come from potential clients who time and again during 1996 had chosen us to manage their money.

In August 1996, a scandal erupted in another part of the company. The manager of Morgan Grenfell's European unit trust, Peter Young, had bought a number of unsuitable investments for the fund and had been dismissed from the company. Although Peter Young had nothing to do with the UK pension fund business and none of my team had anything to do with him or his investments, the bad publicity impacted on the whole of Morgan Grenfell. As a result, we had won virtually no new clients since August and our existing clients were worried and wanted comfort.

At times it was extremely frustrating. Most clients took what we said at face value and then ticked the item off the agenda. Others would ask for a second meeting and sometimes a third to go over the events again and make sure that their assets really were not at risk. After the intense publicity surrounding the Maxwell affair when the Mirror Group Newspapers pension fund was raided by Robert Maxwell, it was inevitable that they were going to be even more concerned than they might otherwise have been. Before that, pension funds were a subject that was hardly ever discussed in the public arena.

I could not blame our clients for being thorough and I would have asked some searching questions if I had been in their place, but nevertheless, I felt demoralized and depressed. We had done our best for the clients and for the firm. The UK pension fund team had not been implicated in any way; it was well organized, with good controls. Yet, in other parts of the bank and in some quarters externally, there seemed to be a feeling that we could not escape being tarred with the same brush.

Before I joined Morgan Grenfell, I had heard a great deal about a particular fund manager there, although I had never actually met him. His name was Adrian Frost. He was regarded as being very good at his job, but a bit of a loner. Because I am known to be forceful in my views, there was general scepticism about how we would get on. Many people in the City were expecting a bust-up. Instead, Adrian and I became very fond of each other and Adrian was my biggest supporter when I was trying to push through reforms in my early days at Morgan Grenfell.

I never did anything at work without conferring with Adrian first. He is wise and I have always valued his judgement. So, in early December, I talked to him about the mood in the team. I was worried that if I felt depressed by the aftermath of the Peter Young affair, the UK equity managers would be feeling even worse. Each UK equity manager has his or her own list of clients and, because 50 to 60 per cent of the average pension fund is invested in UK shares, they are usually the clients' primary point of contact with the company. That meant that they took the brunt of the Peter Young affair, having to explain to clients exactly what had happened and reassure them that their investments were safe.

To make matters worse, some of the UK fund managers had heard the mutterings from other parts of the bank that the whole of asset management should take collective responsibility for what had gone wrong and they were beginning to fear that their bonuses would be cut. To cheer them up and to show them that they were valued, I wanted to invite them and their partners to a Christmas party at my house. There were other Christmas parties, of course, that had been planned for months, but this would be just for the UK equity managers; a thank you from me.

'Do you need to invite partners?' Adrian asked.

I have always thought that the way your partner feels about the organization that you work for is very important. When my husband, Tim, changed jobs in 1996, we had endless conversations about it and he asked me what I thought. He had worked for his old bank for eight years and during that time I had not been invited to one social event. I thought that including partners would encourage a feeling that Morgan Grenfell was a warm, friendly organization to work for. Adrian agreed and so I asked my secretary to send out the invitations.

We usually go away at weekends, but we stayed in London the weekend before the party as I needed to make the house look Christmassy. The previous year, I had bought a beautiful tree but the bottom of it had been far too large for our tree stand. Tim had spent about an hour and a half with a saw in the dining room trying to cut enough off the base of the tree to make it fit the stand.

'Can't we just buy another stand with a bigger hole?' he asked.

'You won't find a stand bigger than that one.'

'Why didn't you ask them to cut the trunk to the right size at the nursery?'

'Because I didn't think of it.'

He sighed, looked at his hands which were threatening

to blister and returned to the hard job of sawing the sap-filled trunk of the Christmas tree.

I had learnt from this experience and got into the car, Christmas-tree stand in hand. I went to see my friend who has a fabulous flower stand on the Fulham Road. He does a great line in Nordic Blue Christmas trees and also has some simple wreaths for the front door.

'I've got just the tree for you,' he declared the moment he saw me and produced a beautifully fresh, nine-foot-tall tree.

'I'll take it if it fits my stand.'

'I'll make it fit your stand,' he said. With four chops of an axe, it was the right size. Oh, I thought, that was where Tim went wrong. On the other hand, it would not have done our wooden floor much good if he had missed with an axe.

I had lots of little helpers to assist in decorating the Christmas tree. I buy a couple of new decorations each year, but always try to keep the tree red and gold. I had also bought a new set of clear fairy lights as the old one had been on the blink the previous year. It did not take long to decorate the tree. Georgie, the eldest, was tall for her age and so she was the most helpful. Alice, who was eight, has always been very artistic and she would take a step back and think before she added a decoration. Serena, who was six, and Rupert, who was three, confined their activities to the lower branches, some of which were groaning under the weight of too many decorations by the time we had finished. A little bit of reorganization was needed, but that would have to wait until they were not looking in case their feelings were hurt.

I remembered that I had six lengths of thick ribbon with bows at the top in a cupboard, so we stapled Christmas cards to them and hung them high on the walls. With the Christmas tree in the bay window of the dining room and the cards hanging on ribbons, all that the room needed was candles. I looked in my candle store. It was running very low.

Sunday opening is a fantastic thing for working women. When we were restricted to shopping on Saturday, it was impossible to get everything done. I know what I like and am a quick buyer. I cannot go shopping with my friends any more as it irritates me that other people tend to take longer to make decisions about buying things. Shop assistants always look astonished when I decide within seconds what I want. Frankly, I do not have much choice. I have so little time to go shopping that if I did not make quick decisions, I would never buy anything.

That afternoon, I took a couple of children and went to a lovely shop which had an outstanding array of candles and Christmas decorations. The children were very keen to assist me in deciding what we should buy, although if they had had their way we would have left with three times as many things as we actually bought. We hung tartan balls on the bay trees outside the front door, put up the wreath and placed gold candles along the mantelpiece. We put white candles in gold holders and set them on the piano. The house was now ready for Christmas and the party.

The only problem was that my party clashed with Tim's office party. There was no way of avoiding this as I could not have thrown a party for sixty people without a cook to help me and this was the only day that she was free. I thought that it was very important that Tim should be at the party if everyone else was bringing partners and so Tim promised that he would not stay out drinking with the boys until the early hours, but would instead make a great personal sacrifice and come back as early as he could.

On the night, the party seemed to be going well. The members of my team thought that it was an excellent idea to have a bonding session and it was great for me to meet some of the wives, husbands, girlfriends and boyfriends whom I had not met before. Everyone was pleased to see Tim when he arrived. Many of them told him how difficult things had been in the wake of the Peter Young affair and said how concerned they had been about whether the team would stick together.

Adrian congratulated me on having come up with the idea of a party. He thought that it had definitely helped to raise spirits. There are always one or two people who stay late and it was as much as I could do to stop myself yawning as I talked to them. Eventually, I staggered to bed at two in the morning. Because I do not drink alcohol I was completely sober, but so tired that I could barely climb the stairs. If I felt like that on 11 December, how was I going to feel by the 24th?

I had an extra burden that year in looking after Georgie. At the end of November she had spent five days in Great Ormond Street Hospital and was discharged with a large quantity of intravenous antibiotics which I had to administer every six hours for ten days. She could have been transferred to our local hospital, but that would have meant that she would have missed ten days of school, which she did not want to do, and I would have been away from work for ten days to keep her company. So, each lunchtime, instead of going home to breastfeed my baby, Antonia, I would climb into a taxi, medical supplies in a bag, and race over to Georgie's school. I was given the use of the science laboratory which seemed like a thoroughly appropriate place to administer the drugs. The netball practice-net was right outside the window and curious girls looked in as I filled syringes with antibiotics, saline and other substances. Some days I could nip back home after this to feed the baby. Other days I did not have time and suffered great discomfort as a result.

At the end of each day, no matter how busy I was, I would have to leave work on time in order to administer Georgie's evening dose. Then the final dose was due at 1 a.m., so I had the choice of either going to sleep and setting the alarm clock or waiting up. I decided to wait up and wrap presents. Though I felt pretty dreadful in the morning, this was my best chance of getting everything done.

We have an enormous family and when you add in all the godchildren and close family friends, buying and wrapping presents is a mammoth task. I always draw up my Christmas present list at the end of October, consulting previous years' lists as I go as I am terrified that one year I might give someone the same thing as the year before. Last year I had seventy children on the list and I have discovered some brilliant mail-order companies which specialize in gifts for children. Dressing-up outfits, personalized stationery, hair bands with individual names on, gardening sets with a fork, a trowel, a small gardening glove and a kneeling pad, soap with a plastic creepy crawly embedded in it, named towels and magnet sets were some of the many things I chose.

As Christmas gets nearer, enormous boxes of toys and gifts arrive every year and the children eye them curiously. I wait until they have gone to bed and then tear them open, barely able to remember what I ordered for which child. I try to wrap as I go, otherwise I know that one of the children is going to discover them and spoil the surprise. Choosing presents for my own children is particularly difficult as four out of the five have birthdays near the end of the year. We start off with Georgie on 19 October and then there are birthdays and parties every two weeks until Christmas. I planned it that way as I wanted to be on maternity leave over Christmas. By the time I got to the fifth, Antonia, I thought it was time for a change. She was born in the summer.

Then there are all the carol concerts. I love carols and embarrass my family by singing with great gusto. Often Georgie nudges me and tells me not to sing so loudly. Even Rupert's nursery school had a carol concert that Christmas. The children looked like little angels and some of them sang their hearts out. Rupert sang intermittently and fidgeted a great deal. But, no matter how many carol concerts we went to, Rupert could not get enough. Every single night after I had read him his story, I had to put a tape of carols on for him and every morning he would come down to breakfast humming 'Little Donkey', his favourite. He still sometimes asks for his carols tape when I am putting him to bed and I try to explain that it is bad luck to listen to carols outside the festive season. He thinks this is a pretty poor excuse, but he generally gives in. Occasionally, I wake up in the morning to hear 'The Holly and the Ivy' and 'Little Donkey' floating down through the floorboards in the summer.

The party that I had had for my team had reinforced each person's feelings of loyalty to the team itself, but unfortunately it had done nothing to overcome the anger that many of them felt towards Morgan Grenfell as a result of the Peter Young affair and the way our business and the firm's reputation had been affected. A few days after the party, one of my senior colleagues said to me that he thought I should know that there were a number of people who were unhappy and were thinking of leaving. There were two things that might stop them. The first was to increase my own power in the organization, which would allow us to make sure that the other divisions were as tightly run as the UK pension fund business. The second was to give them more money, as some of the younger fund managers felt that they were underpaid relative to their peers in other organizations. In effect he was issuing me with an ultimatum.

I could not react immediately to this. I knew I had to spend some time thinking about what the right strategy might be. The one thing I was determined to do was hold the team together. We had done so well and it would be a tragedy if it was to fall apart as a result of something we had no part in.

I decided that the first thing I would do was to go and see my boss, Robert Smith. Robert was a Scottish accountant who had recently joined asset management from the development capital division and taken on the role of Chief Executive. We had a good rapport and I liked his direct approach. My first aim would be to persuade him that the controls and disciplines that existed in the UK business had to be imposed across the whole organization. At the same time, I would try to obtain generous pay increases for the younger fund managers, knowing perfectly well that we would lose staff if we did not pay market rates. I then had to ask myself what I would do if I failed to achieve this. I began to think about whether I might be able to persuade Morgan Grenfell to sell the UK pension fund business, for which I was responsible, either to the management or to another bank. It seemed like a fanciful idea, but I thought it was worth exploring.

I discussed all of this with three of my senior colleagues. We all wanted to hold the team together and we all preferred to remain part of Morgan Grenfell. None the less, they agreed with me that it might be worth trying to persuade the senior management to sell the business if all else failed. One of the members of my team had previously worked at ABN Amro, a Dutch bank, and he believed that they may be willing to finance a purchase. He suggested that we should talk to them and rang his old boss at ABN Amro to arrange it. As a senior director of Morgan Grenfell,

I was concerned about this and did not want to breach my contractual obligations. I sought legal advice on what I could and could not do and say and I followed it to the letter.

My last day in the office before Christmas was 20 December. The day before you go on holiday is always hectic and it was especially so that day. I had to distribute cards and chocolates to all the secretaries, check through all the Christmas cards that I had been sent to make sure I had not forgotten anybody, look through all the outstanding correspondence on my desk and delegate anything that I knew I would not have time to deal with myself. Everything had to be finished in time to take Georgie to Great Ormond Street at 1.30 p.m.

As my last and most important task of the day, I was due to see Sir John Craven. He was the Chairman of Deutsche Morgan Grenfell, which owned Morgan Grenfell Asset Management, and the most senior person in London, and I wanted to enlist his help in getting proper pay rises for the younger members of my team. Before that, I went to the meeting with ABN Amro. I explained that things had been difficult at Morgan Grenfell after the Peter Young affair and that I was anxious to hold the team together. I said that I did not think that it was impossible that Morgan Grenfell might consider an offer for the UK pension fund business. I told them that I was not trying to do anything underhand or looking to force Morgan Grenfell to sell at a knockdown price. I did stress that, if I could hold the team together at Morgan Grenfell, that was the preferred route. The interests of the clients were foremost in my mind. After fifteen minutes, I raced off to see Sir John Craven and put ABN Amro out of my mind until January.

Georgie and I arrived home from Great Ormond Street at 6.30 p.m. and the plan was to drive down to Hampshire that evening. I looked at the enormous pile of presents under the tree and tried to imagine how I was going to fit them all in. We would have to take two cars. Tim could take three children and a small number of presents in his car and I could take two children and the rest of the presents in my car, which has a roof box. I balanced precariously on the side of the car and swung the bags into the top and then Tim and I closed the roof box and eyed the rest of the presents.

'You should get the children to open some of their presents before we go,' Tim said. The children were delighted at this unexpected treat, but it was not such a good idea after all.

'I want to take it down to the country and play with it there,' Serena said clasping an enormous box filled with drawing things.

'Well, you can't,' I replied.

'Why not?'

'Because you've got hundreds of other presents to open down there and you can play with them.' Tears began to roll down her face and my attempts to jolly her along completely failed. The doorbell rang. It was John Richards, an old friend of mine from the City who is Alice's godfather.

'I know you're going any minute, but I thought that I would just pop round with some presents for the children.'

After John and I had kissed each other goodbye and exchanged Christmas greetings, I set off in the direction of the A3. The children fell asleep within minutes. Once I was on the dual carriageway, my eyes became heavy. I could not imagine how I was going to get to Hampshire without falling asleep at the wheel and crashing. Tim had left a few minutes before me and was already out of sight. I would have to stop if I really could not stay awake. Somehow I hung in there, holding the steering wheel very tightly and leaning slightly forward. I turned the heat down. At 10.30 p.m., we rolled into the drive. Tim and I carried the children to their beds and left the presents unpacked until the morning. The only thing that had to come inside was the Christmas cake.

I love cooking and I always make the Christmas cake. Tim had an aunt who baked wonderful cakes and I inherited a massive mixing bowl from her when she died. I find it very satisfying mixing all the ingredients together: sultanas, raisins, currants, candied peel, cherries, chopped almonds, ground almonds, dark brown sugar, flour, eggs and the secret ingredient of a moist Christmas cake – two grated cooking apples. My arm aches by the time I have finished. Of course, I always intend to make the cake in November, but end up doing it a few days before Christmas.

I made the cake on my one free December evening and then started to plan what I would cook over the holidays. I got out all my favourite cookery books and began to put together some menus. My parents, my grandmother and my brother's family are all vegetarian, so this was a complicating factor. I also had to plan where and when I was going to do the shopping. Not in London as the car would be packed with children and presents, but in Hampshire with no nanny it would be difficult to avoid taking at least some of the children with me. Whenever I take them, I end up with all sorts of things that I never knew I wanted and the whole process takes twice as long as when I go by myself. I decided that the morning after we arrived in Hampshire, I would leave home at 8 a.m. and arrive at Sainsbury's as the doors opened. Needless to say I overslept, but eventually I returned with two trolley-loads of goodies. Tim looked after three of the children and I took the younger two with me.

You always forget something. This year I forgot about the Christmas tree for Hampshire. Usually I go down the week before Christmas, but this year I had not been able to and so we had no tree. Tim volunteered to go to the local nursery, only to return saying that they had sold out. I rang my parents who live near Chichester and my mother found a tree which she delivered the next day. When I unwrapped it all the needles fell off. It had obviously been cut some time before and left in a very dry place. I was at my wits' end. We had to have a tree. Eventually we found one, very full but rather short. I had the disk drive from an old computer in the cellar and so I wrapped it in red crêpe paper and put the tree on top of it to make it look taller. When we arranged the presents round it, the disk drive was completely lost from sight.

The next job was to make marzipan and put it on the

Christmas cake. The following day it would be ready to ice and then I would have to find some fresh holly with red berries to decorate it.

On Christmas Eve, the children woke up at 6 a.m. in a state of high excitement. We always open our presents on Christmas Eve as my Polish mother used to do as a child. I think it is much more exciting for the children to open their presents in the dark, gathered round the Christmas tree in their dressing gowns and slippers.

'Mummy! Mummy! I want to ask you something.' I opened my eyes to see Rupert standing next to our bed. I had not gone to sleep until 1.30 a.m. as I had been making puddings and dealing with the Christmas cake.

'What do you want, darling?'

'When are Granny and Grandpa coming?'

'They'll be here at tea-time.'

'Oh.' He paused and stuck his muslin, which he still sleeps with, in his mouth. 'When is Father Christmas coming?'

'Tonight before you go to bed, we will put some mince pies on a plate and pour out a glass of sherry. Then we will put it on the mantelpiece and when Father Christmas comes down the chimney, he will eat the mince pies and drink the sherry and then he will come and put your presents in your stocking.' Rupert thought for a moment.

'Won't he burn his bottom if he comes down the chimney?'

'Don't worry, darling. The fire will be out by the time he comes.' While we were talking, the baby woke up and began to cry. There was no hope of going back to sleep. My eyes felt heavy and my bones ached as I got out of bed.

I had to go to the shops to buy a few last-minute things that morning. Then I wrapped a couple of presents that were left over from the night before when I had finally succumbed to tiredness after finishing the cooking. I checked the sitting room. It looked very pretty with the tree in the corner and all the presents around it. I decided to organize the presents into piles. It would be easier later when everyone came into the room to open them.

My parents and my grandmother arrived at about 4 p.m. Our nanny, Joan Buckfield, had come down to spend Christmas with us and so we were ten for supper excluding the baby. Vegetarian lasagne and salad was on the menu for the grown-ups and lamb for the children. They go to a school which only serves vegetarian food and they eat it grudgingly. When they have the choice, they would rather eat meat. My parents brought their two golden retrievers and their two dachshunds and the children were much more interested in the dogs than they were in eating their food. Only when I produced meringues and brandy snaps filled with whipped cream did their attention turn away from the dogs. Soon they were covered in cream and had very sticky fingers.

'Can you see a star in the sky?' my grandmother asked Georgie. Georgie looked out of the window. It was a very dark evening.

'I can't see any stars.'

'Well, you can't open your presents then,' I said.

'Don't be silly, Mummy.'

'The tradition is that you can open your presents when you see the first star.'

'Well what happens if there are lots of clouds in the sky and you can't see any stars then?' Georgie was getting cross.

'Then you can't open your presents until Christmas Day.' The children looked horrified at the prospect of having to wait until the morning to open the presents. 'Don't worry! We wouldn't be that mean to you,' I said and a look of relief spread across their faces.

My mother had added another enormous pile of presents to those already around the tree. I quickly sorted them out and put them on all the individual piles and then called the children. They tore the paper off each present and there were shrieks of excitement.

'I really wanted one of these! Georgie, look what I've got! Thank you, thank you, thank you, Mummy,' said Serena (known to all the family as Mouse). She is always very appreciative when she is given presents and is delighted with every little item. Rupert was completely overwhelmed. At just three it was the first time that he could really appreciate what was going on. There were so many toys and books and he wanted to play with or read each one as he unwrapped it. Georgie is very organized. As she took the paper off her presents, she put it in one pile and the presents in another. Alice is the most untidy of our children. She was barely visible as she sat in the middle of an enormous heap of paper and presents.

I got the black plastic rubbish bags out and started picking up bits of paper. All those hours that I had spent wrapping the presents and it took but a few minutes to unwrap them all. It was difficult to tear the children away from their new toys and games.

'Let's go and get some mince pies and sherry ready for Father Christmas,' I said. Only Rupert seemed at all interested in doing this. We put them up on the mantelpiece and then I suggested that it was time for him to go to bed and hang his stocking up.

'I don't want to. I want to play with my toys.'

'You can play with them all day tomorrow, darling, and you will have all the toys from Father Christmas as well.' He started to cry and thought that I was being extremely mean to him. 'The girls are going to bed now too, darling. Let's go and choose some of your new toys for you to take up with you and we will tell them that they have got to go to bed as well.'

It took hours to get them all to go to bed and it was still longer before they were all asleep. Whilst I had been dealing with the children, my mother and father had done all the washing up and I came down to a sparkling kitchen. We said goodnight and they went back home to Chichester with not many hours left before they would be welcoming all of us to their house for Christmas Day.

I came across the photographs from last Christmas the other day when I was packing things up before moving house. We all look tired, run down and strained. My father had had open-heart surgery five months earlier, just before he and my mother were due to move from Cheshire to Chichester. In the photographs, he is very thin and frail. My mother worried about him a great deal during those few months after the operation and the move on top of everything else took a lot out of her. I had a small baby and had had a hard time at work. Tim had started a new job and had been working very long hours during his first few months. And Georgie was just getting over a serious infection.

At the time, however, it seemed like any other Christmas. It was exciting to be celebrating it in my parents' new house which is ancient and labyrinthine with towers and turrets and rooms hidden away at the top of small spiral staircases. Even though she is a vegetarian and would not dream of eating a mouthful of turkey herself, my mother accepts that her grandchildren are die-hard carnivores and she cooked them a magnificent meal with all the trimmings. The Christmas pudding was made with vegetarian suet, but they could not tell the difference. That evening I did not have to argue with the children about going to bed. They were all so tired that they were begging me to allow them to skip their baths and go straight to sleep. Tim and I were exhausted too.

The rest of our two weeks in Hampshire passed very rapidly. We had bought the house five years earlier and it had been a wreck. No one had lived in it for years and there was damp and rot everywhere. The site was so beautiful, though, that Tim and I fell in love with it. It took three years to restore the house and it now provided a peaceful retreat from our frenzied London existence. We saw many friends and I spent a good deal of the time in the kitchen either preparing food or washing up, but I enjoyed it nevertheless. It was a change from my usual routine. I did not think about work, my unhappy fund managers or ABN Amro once during those two weeks. I did not have a spare minute to do so.

I returned to work on 2 January to find that one of my colleagues had arranged a meeting with ABN Amro for the next day. They said that they may be prepared to contemplate buying the business themselves if it was for sale. We met again on 7 January so that they could explain their strategy for their asset management business. I was in Birmingham on business the following day, but got a message to say that I should go to the Lanesborough Hotel in Knightsbridge on my return. I had no idea why I was being summoned there, but I went and found that I was meeting with one of the most senior people from ABN Amro's main board who was over from the Netherlands. I was a little surprised to see him and a little embarrassed. He thought that it was unlikely that Morgan Grenfell would sell its UK pension fund company, but he said that ABN Amro would be very interested in employing me as an individual to run the whole of its asset management business in London.

I felt confused after this meeting. I did not want to leave Morgan Grenfell. Other people had intimated that they were considering leaving and I was the one who was trying to stop them by investigating various ways of keeping the team together. Now a major European bank was trying to recruit me to run its business. With a new baby and a sick child, the last thing I wanted to do was to take on a job like that. I was making good progress with my preferred plan. The pay increases for the junior staff were likely to come as a pleasant surprise to them and I knew that would help to keep them. My senior colleagues were giving me a great deal of support and, as a result, on Friday 10 January, Robert Smith offered me the title of Managing Director of Morgan Grenfell Asset Management. Previously I had just been in charge of the UK pension fund business, but now I was to have responsibility for international pension funds and unit trusts as well. I had thus fulfilled both the conditions of the ultimatum and felt cheerful and confident about my team's future at Morgan Grenfell. I rang ABN Amro to tell them I was very flattered that they wanted to employ me, but that I did not wish to take the discussions any further.

The events of 14 January 1997 will be etched on my memory for ever. The alarm went off at 6.40 a.m. Tim turned it off and, as usual, rolled over and went back to sleep. I lay in that half awake, half asleep state that most people experience on cold winter mornings, trying to remember the contents of my diary, working out whether I needed to look smart or very smart and whether I had to leap out of bed or could take my time. I realized that I had a prospective client coming in at 9 a.m. and I had not yet looked at the document that I was to present.

Within minutes I had brushed my teeth, dressed and done my make-up. I grabbed the baby, dressed her and fed her. On my way down the stairs to kiss the children goodbye, little voices began to shout, 'It's Mummy!' With the baby safely in her highchair, my hands were free to give each of my other four children a hug and a kiss before I departed. As I kissed the first, the others were shouting

'Kiss me, Mummy!' and as I kissed the next, there came further shouts of 'You haven't kissed me!' This was the normal morning routine. When I had kissed each child at least three times, I was allowed to leave the room.

As I drove down Kensington High Street on that fateful day, I listened to the *Today* programme on Radio 4. The presenters were, as usual, taking an aggressive stance with every interviewee whether he or she was an unknown figure, there to give an expert opinion, or a top politician. I drove through Knightsbridge, past Buckingham Palace and down to Parliament Square, and then on to the Embankment with the City in full view looking splendid in the early morning light.

As I sat waiting at one of the road blocks that was set up after the IRA bombed Bishopsgate, my thoughts turned to the presentation. I was not nervous as I spent a great deal of time explaining how we went about our business. The man I was seeing was acting on behalf of a large local council and was checking us out thoroughly before recommending us to his trustees.

Once at my desk, I flicked through the document and made a few notes. Then I discovered that the colleague who was meant to be making the presentation with me was not there because his wife had the flu and he had to stay at home to look after her. I was not impressed. I could not imagine expecting Tim to stay at home to look after me if I had the flu, especially if he was meant to be making an important presentation. I went round the team and persuaded Adrian to stand in. He shared my irritation with our colleague, but understood that it was an important prospective client and that we had to put on a good show. I threw him a document and told him that he had five minutes to go through it.

Soon we were in the meeting-room taking copious notes on the history of the fund as the prospective client talked. Our marketing director, Rufus Warner, was with us. After about half an hour, the prospective client was ready to hear what we had to say. I could sense that he was interested in the long presentation rather than the potted version and I could happily have talked all day. He had originally said that he would only be with us for an hour, but now he told me that he had more time if it was needed.

A few minutes later, I was in full flow, telling him what a wonderful organization Morgan Grenfell was and how much we had achieved over the previous five years, when the meeting-room telephone rang. This was not uncommon, but usually the call was for the guest. Rufus picked up the telephone while I continued to talk. He caught my eye and I stopped.

'Robert Smith would like to see you,' he said with a look of surprise on his face.

'Tell him that I'm in the middle of making a presentation and I'll see him when I have finished.' Rufus relayed this brief message, the coffee cups were refilled and I continued.

I thought nothing of Robert Smith's request to see me on that Tuesday morning. I assumed that he must have thought I was in an internal meeting which could be interrupted. At 11 a.m., our guest left the room for a few minutes saying that he thought we would be finished by noon, so I asked my secretary to relay this information to

Robert Smith. At 11.20 a.m., Robert Smith's secretary rang and insisted on talking to me. Although I explained again that I was doing a new business presentation and would be finished by noon, she said that Robert Smith had to see me urgently and I had no choice but to go. I wondered what could possibly be so urgent.

I ran down the stairs to the fund management floor. Robert Smith's secretary greeted me with a smile and redirected me to a ground-floor meeting room. I opened the door to find Robert Smith waiting for me with Martyn Drain, the personnel director. I had had a meeting with them the previous week about the pay review, so I thought they must be about to discuss that. I began to explain why I had not come down earlier, but Robert Smith interrupted me.

'Nicola, we have asked you to come here because we have decided to suspend you. I have a letter here which outlines the reasons why and a more detailed letter setting out the allegations against you will be sent to you shortly. You will remain at home on full pay until we have completed an internal investigation and we would like you to come to 23 Great Winchester Street on Friday at 8 a.m. where you will be given an opportunity to give your side of the story. Martyn and I will be present and you can bring a colleague with you.' I tried to cut in as he was saying this, but he continued, speaking slowly and deliberately. At the end he said that he did not wish to discuss my side of the story then as I would have the opportunity to put my case on Friday. I asked if anyone would know that I had been suspended and he said that he had to put a note round otherwise my colleagues would wonder where I had disappeared to. Despite his initial determination not to enter into a discussion about the rights and wrongs of suspending me, Robert Smith listened as I told him why he should reverse his decision. I said that I was completely committed to Morgan Grenfell. I had always been completely committed. All I had been trying to do was to hold my business together. I pleaded with him to listen to me, but he got up and left the room.

I stayed in the room with Martyn Drain for about ten minutes after Robert Smith left. Neither of us said anything at first. I could not believe what had just happened and fingered the envelope that I had been given nervously. Martyn looked very tense and was clearly hoping that it would all be over quickly. I quizzed him about whether I would be given a genuine opportunity to put my case if I attended on Friday and he insisted that I would. When I said that it looked as though my career at Morgan Grenfell was over, he said that there was a real possibility that I would be reinstated on Friday. If I was so certain that I had done nothing wrong, then that would come out in the internal inquiry.

There was another uncomfortable pause and then Martyn Drain asked me to go upstairs, get my things, hand him my security card and leave the building. A few minutes later, I found myself standing outside the front door of the building in a state of shock. I began to shake, but I could not cry. My cheeks were burning and I started to feel sick. I had worked for Morgan Grenfell for five and a half years. I had given everything I had to the organization and turned an ailing business into one of the most successful in its field. I had found the Peter Young affair extremely difficult to handle and had felt very angry about the damage that had been done to the reputation of the firm, but I had defended the actions that had been taken to clients even though I disagreed with some of them. I could not believe that I would be reinstated whatever Martyn Drain had said. I was certain that my career at Morgan Grenfell had come to an end.

two

I had a pretty conventional upbringing. My parents are still married after thirty-eight years together. They were part of a generation that believed it was socially irresponsible to have more than two children, since world population was exploding perhaps beyond control. They had their two children, a girl and a boy. Both were healthy and seemed reasonably bright.

My mother had an extremely dramatic start to life. She was born in Warsaw in January 1939, eight months before Hitler invaded Poland. On 1 September 1939, my grandfather went out shooting and returned to be told the news by my grandmother, who had already changed for the cocktail party they were going to that evening. My grandparents, both journalists, had followed the rise of Adolf Hitler closely and they decided there was no time to lose. Hitler was already showing anti-Semitic tendencies and my grandmother was Jewish. They had to get out of Poland. My grandmother grabbed clothes for the three of them and put my mother and her two Papillon dogs in the car. My grandfather drove them as fast as he could towards the border with the Ukraine. Soon they ran out of petrol and it was impossible to buy any more. They swapped the car for a horse and cart.

Two days later, they finally crossed the Soviet border and were put in a makeshift refugee camp. My grandfather had to work down a tin mine in order to earn a few roubles each day to pay for bread, drinking water and other limited supplies. My grandmother, who speaks several languages, acted as an interpreter between the refugees and the camp authorities and, in return, the family received special rations from time to time. As a result, my mother was stronger than most of the other children and so, when an epidemic of cholera hit the camp, she remained healthy.

When the Hitler–Stalin pact fell apart, my grandparents were liberated. They and a number of other Poles decided to go to Palestine where there was a large British presence. They travelled overland through Turkey and Syria. When they reached Bethlehem, they found a French convent and the nuns agreed to look after my mother, who was almost three. Her first language became French and she was adored by the nuns. She has vivid memories of them gently trying to persuade her to eat her *pain au chocolat* each morning at breakfast. They thought this would be a treat, but she found the sweet taste alien after almost two years of eating tasteless food in the camp. My grandparents visited my mother when they could, but were comforted by the fact that she was safe with the nuns.

My grandparents went on to Cairo and joined a group of Polish soldiers who were fighting with the British. My grandfather became one of General Anders's press officers and my grandmother continued her work as an interpreter. Just before my mother's fifth birthday, my grandmother had some leave and she wanted to take my mother from Bethlehem to Cairo. Foreign children were not allowed into a war zone until they were five and so my grandmother had some documents forged which changed my mother's birthday from 5 January 1939 to 5 December 1938. To this day, my mother celebrates her birthday in December.

At the end of the war, my grandparents were sent to Kenya by the army and decided to settle there when peace was declared. My grandfather occasionally talked about returning to Poland, but my grandmother was shocked that the British had gone to war with Germany over the invasion of Poland and then had handed it over to the Soviet Union. She now had two children and she did not want to take them behind the Iron Curtain. Eventually my grandfather returned, leaving my grandmother and their children in Kenya.

When my mother was nineteen, she came to the UK to stay with some friends in Nottingham. My father was working at Raleigh Industries, the bicycle manufacturer, and it was his boss with whom my mother was staying. They met and fell in love. My mother had to return to Kenya and when she stepped off the boat, she was handed a telegram asking her to marry him. She was married at the age of twenty and had me when she was twenty-one.

As a result of her unsettled childhood, my mother was determined to give us a secure upbringing. We had lots of love. When we were away at school, she used to write to us every day and when we were at university, we would speak on the telephone every other day. When I went to school in the US for a few months, the telephone bill was six times as large as usual. My brother and I still talk to our parents several times each week.

There are two and a half years between my brother and me. He was born at home and I remember his arrival very clearly. My mother went into labour late on a June evening and her cries of pain woke me. I went down to the sitting room and sat with Dilys, my nanny, looking at books on the floor. A wild thunderstorm was raging outside and I was frightened, but the excitement of a new baby arriving overrode those fears. At about 2 a.m., my father came down and said that Dilys could bring me upstairs to see my brother, Christopher. As I walked into the room, I saw my mother lying on the bed with her eyes closed and an oxygen mask over her face. My heart jumped, but then I saw a blond, chubby babe being bathed in a red washing-up bowl and ran over to touch him. I adored him immediately. Because he was so fat, my mother nicknamed him Bumble and the family still calls him by that name.

In 1966, we moved to the Wirral, near Liverpool, where my father had been born. We moved because he had been invited to join the family firm which was called Roy Wilson, Dickson Ltd. My grandfather was still working and the staff used to call him Mr Dudley and my father Mr Michael. When my grandfather retired, my father became Managing Director and retained that title for thirty years.

I was sent to a girls' prep school where we did a great deal of painting and knitting. When my brother was old enough to go to proper school, he was sent to Kingsmead in Hoylake. I went round the school with my parents and saw that there was a large art room, an enormous gymnasium with huge ropes hanging from the ceiling, a large playground and then acres and acres of playing fields. This was much better than my school and I wanted to go there too. Kingsmead had recently started to take the occasional sister of a pupil and they agreed to take me.

The school was run by David and Dorothy Watts, who were devout Christians and extremely kind people. They were both prominent in school life, were always available if a pupil had a problem and took care to instil the right values in us. They encouraged a high degree of academic success, but we also learnt the value of music, art, drama and sport. Although it was a very competitive environment, everyone was encouraged to try their hand at something. I was keen on athletics and, in particular, high jumping. I had an unfair advantage as I was very tall for my age and towered over most of the boys, so it was not a surprise when I won the high jumping medal two years running. I was also in the school choir and we used to take part in competitions all over the country. We even went to Switzerland one year to participate in an international singing competition.

Whilst I was very happy at Kingsmead, my brother was not. Even the best schools do not suit everyone. My parents were very worried about Christopher and had many conversations with Mrs Watts about him. Being a sensitive soul, they thought that he would do better in a smaller school and so they sent him to a prep school up in the Welsh hills called Heronwater. My mother was a little apprehensive about sending him to boarding school at nine, but there were no local schools that she and my father thought would be suitable for him. The day he arrived, he was asked what instrument he was going to play. He learned the piano, trumpet and organ and later won a music scholarship to Stowe School. It seemed that this had been the missing element in his life and once he discovered his musical talent, he became a different child.

At the age of twelve, I was sent away to Cheltenham Ladies' College. My grandfather's second wife, who is also my godmother, had gone there, as had Dorothy Watts's daughter, Margie. My father wanted me to have the best education available and he believed that, by sending me to Cheltenham, he would be giving me this. The fact that I was a girl was of no consequence. He believed that the most important thing he could give his children was a good education. Cheltenham was academically strong and he believed that I would find it a stimulating environment.

By the time I left Kingsmead, it had taken in a few more girls, but it was still predominantly a boys' school. The fact that there were so few girls meant that everyone knew who we were and we had a special status in the school. Every year, I was Mary in the school nativity play and in other dramatic productions the other girls and I always featured prominently. We were all academically able and won prizes at Speech Day. We were slightly apart from the boys. We were different and we were used to being treated as such.

Cheltenham could not have been a starker contrast and I hated the place from the moment I arrived. I was not special any more. I was just one of a thousand girls. There was nothing to do at weekends and boredom gave way to bitchiness as we sat in our houses hour after hour come rain or shine.

Looking back, I think there are two reasons why the weekends were so bleak and boring. First there was a pervasive and overriding fear amongst the staff that one of us might get pregnant. Cheltenham is not a campus school and the boarding houses are spread across the town. Thus, as soon as we stepped out of the door, we were in dangerous territory. The safest thing to do was to confine us to our houses all weekend. Activities could have been arranged, but most of the staff had the weekends off and we were left with our housemistresses. In boys' boarding schools, it is common for housemasters to be married with their own children, so there is something of a family atmosphere. At Cheltenham, the housemistresses were either divorcees or spinsters and had no families living with them. The result was a feeling that they were in charge of us like warders in a prison.

In addition, we were permanently hungry. The food that we did get was well cooked, but there was just not enough of it. We would return to our houses after morning lessons to a reasonable lunch, but in the evening all we would get were a couple of spoonfuls of either baked beans or spaghetti hoops and a piece of toast. We were required to dress for dinner and most of us would come down to the dining room in full-length skirts. The incongruity was ridiculous.

I spent much of my time at Cheltenham thinking of ways to circumvent the harsh regime. One day, I came across the deputy housemistress's hiding place for the keys to the back door. I told two of my friends and we decided to go out, under cover of darkness, and buy fish and chips. This was an unbelievably daring thing to do and we were really worried that someone would catch us as we put the key in the lock and slipped out of the door. I have never liked fish and chips much, but they tasted absolutely delicious that night. We made several night-time forays until one night we found that the key had been moved. Maybe the lingering smell of chips in the laundry room had raised suspicion.

On another occasion, I decided to make soup in the dormitory. I found a broken music stand and an old Quality Street tin and hid them in the top of the wardrobe. I was able to obtain some candles, matches and packets of chicken noodle soup. I told my friends about my plan and they were amazed by the audacity of it. That night, I got the music stand down, twisted it into a tripod and placed the open tin on top. I lit a candle and dropped wax on to the lid of the tin before setting each of the candles in position. Then I gently moved the lid under the tripod and mixed the soup. It took about five minutes for the first bubble to appear and then the soup began to simmer. We all sat around the strange cooking apparatus in a state of high excitement, peering into the tin to see if the soup would really cook. Eventually, I judged that it was ready. There were nine of us, but we only had two mugs and so we passed them among us, declaring it to be the most delicious soup we had ever tasted. A couple of days later, the deputy housemistress did a dorm search while we were in class and confiscated the equipment. We were all summoned to see the housemistress, Mrs Adrian-Vallance (known as A-V) in her study. We had already considered this eventuality and we had agreed that we would all stare at her feet.

'I was absolutely horrified when I heard what had been found in your dormitory this morning. Do you realize that you could have burnt the house down and that everyone might have been killed?' said A-V with an extremely grave expression on her face. We stared at her feet and were silent. There was an awkward pause and A-V began to shuffle slightly and looked at her feet, clearly wondering if there was something wrong with her shoes. 'Don't you have anything to say for yourselves?'

There was another pause and then I said, 'We are very sorry, Mrs Adrian-Vallance.'

'You had better go and do your homework,' she said and we filed out of the room trying not to look at each other in case we giggled.

From the very beginning, I had told my parents that I hated Cheltenham and did not want to stay there. They insisted that I should give it a chance, but at the end of every holiday I would develop a sore throat or an earache and our family doctor began to think it was psychosomatic. After almost two years, I could stand it no longer. At the beginning of the summer term of my second year, I ran away.

Once each term we were allowed out in pairs to go shopping on the Promenade, the main shopping street in Cheltenham. I took a pair of jeans with me and told the girl who was with me that I wanted to buy a top to go with them. We were meant to stay together at all times, but we agreed that we would get more done if we parted company for half an hour. I disappeared into a shop, bought a yellow top to go with the jeans, stuffed my uniform into a carrier bag and headed for the bus station. My best friend from home had recently moved to a village near Banbury and my plan was to go to her mother as I thought that she would be the only person who would really understand how unhappy I was. But there was no direct bus. I would have to go via Oxford.

As the bus made its way towards Oxford, I knew the alarm would already have been raised. The police had probably been informed of my disappearance and the bus station was one of the first places they would go. Someone would tell them that they had seen a dark-haired girl wearing jeans getting on to the Oxford bus. There were bound to be policemen waiting for me in Oxford. One-third of the way there, I got off the bus in the middle of nowhere. I decided that I would spend the night in some woods and think about what to do the next day. I had a small amount of food with me and a couple of cans of drink.

I walked from the bus stop towards the woods, passing through a small village. There was no one about, but still I worried that someone could have seen me through a window as I walked past. I found a hiding place in a thicket of bushes and settled down. It was the end of April and, although it had been a reasonably warm day, it was beginning to get cold. I got my school uniform out of my carrier bag and put the jacket on to keep warm.

I must have sat there for over an hour. I began to imagine what might happen to me if I stayed in the wood overnight. If I went to sleep, someone might come and murder me. I decided that I would go back to Cheltenham and get a train. If I was confronted by the police at the station, I would just have to persuade them to let me go home.

I waited a long time for a bus on the main road, but finally one came. It actually said 'Not in Service', but I waved my hand frantically in the air and, kindly, the driver stopped. Strictly speaking, he was not meant to take passengers, but he promised to give me a lift as long as I did not tell anyone. We arrived back at the bus station in Cheltenham, which was surprisingly free of policemen. I took a taxi to the railway station. There was no evidence of police there either, so I bought a ticket for Liverpool. The next train was in fifteen minutes.

Five minutes before the train was due to arrive, I spotted two policemen coming over the footbridge from the station entrance and then down the steps to the platform where I was sitting. I looked in the other direction and pretended that I had not seen them, until they were standing right in front of me. One of them asked me my name. I did not reply.

'We are looking for a girl who looks just like you,' the other one said. 'Can I look in your bag?'

'Do you have a search warrant?' I asked. He made a grab for the bag and I threw it at him and pelted down the platform. I could not see any way out, so I climbed some railings and found myself in a quiet residential area behind the station. I ran as fast as I could, not knowing where I was going. I could hear the policemen's boots thumping behind me. Eventually, I tripped on a paving stone and fell flat on my face. The policemen grabbed one arm each and frogmarched me back to the railway station. I was furious. I was sure they had no right to stop me going home if I wanted to.

As we walked back along the platform, the train pulled in. I struggled again, but the policemen continued to pull me along. I was led out of the main entrance to the station and, to my surprise, I was not put into a police car, but was instead pushed into the front seat of a large brown Rover. A smiling face greeted me.

'Nicola, my dear. We were so concerned about you.' It was Miss Hampshire, the headmistress of Cheltenham Ladies' College. A wave of guilt came over me, followed by fear. I had, no doubt, caused a great deal of concern, not least to my poor parents who had probably thought that I had been abducted and that they might never see me again. What was I going to say when I saw them? How was I going to explain my actions to Miss Hampshire?

Miss Hampshire drove me to her house, telling me that she would like me to spend the night with her rather than return to my house. She did not reprimand me in any way. Instead, she made me some supper and let me sit on the sofa in her drawing room with her small dog on my lap while she was in the kitchen. The fact that she was being so kind made me feel even more guilty. After supper, she showed me to a pretty bedroom and I was asleep the moment my head hit the pillow.

The next day, my parents arrived. They both looked worried and pale. My mother barely spoke to me and I could see that she was not at all pleased with me. We talked to Miss Hampshire for a while. I said that I hated Chelten- ham and that I did not want to return to the school. Miss Hampshire's kindness finally gave way to anger and she said that I was a very spoilt child who had caused a lot of anxiety to many people. I could not understand why it was deemed to be a crime to be unhappy. My brother had been very unhappy at Kingsmead whereas I had adored it. That was proof in my mind that no school can suit everyone. It was agreed that the best thing would be for me to go home for a few days and Miss Hampshire would speak to my father on the telephone about what should be done with me.

On the long drive home, my mother could no longer contain her fury. She said that I had ruined my academic career. She insisted that she and my father knew how unhappy I was and had made plans to discuss the matter with Miss Hampshire before I ran away. I sank into my seat and was overwhelmed with depression. I knew that if I had only waited, the situation could have been resolved without all this fuss. Now Miss Hampshire would probably try and expel me and my mother was convinced that if that happened, none of the local schools would take me. In the end, my father's outstanding negotiating skills avoided an expulsion and I was withdrawn from the school.

There was an excellent school near us which all the bright local girls went to. It was called Birkenhead High School and it was a member of the Girls' Public Day School Trust. When it was decided that I would not return to

Cheltenham, I went to see Miss Freda Kellett, the headmistress, and told her the whole story. Although I had not been expelled, my mother was still sceptical about the chances of Birkenhead taking me and I was determined to prove her wrong. Miss Kellett was very sympathetic. Even though I had not taken the entrance exam, she said that I could come and spend a week at the school and, if I liked it, I could stay. I was over the moon. I went for a week and stayed until the end of my school career.

I was very happy during the three years that I was at Birkenhead High School. The school was not particularly strong on music and art, but had a good drama teacher, which meant that I could do some acting which I loved. The fact that it was a day school meant that I could do outside activities and I took singing lessons, amongst other things. My parents were surprised at how much calmer I was and it became clear that Cheltenham just had not been the right school for me. One of the things I hated most about Cheltenham was the bitchiness of the girls and, not knowing any better, I blamed it on the girls themselves. The girls at Birkenhead High School were completely different: open and friendly in a way I associated with the boys at Kingsmead. I realized then that the reason the Cheltenham girls were bitchy was because they were in a completely artificial environment, shut inside with nothing better to do than turn their thwarted energy against each other.

While I was away at Cheltenham, my father stood for Parliament as a Liberal in both the General Elections of 1974. This had caused a bit of a stir as our constituency was represented by the then Speaker of the House of

Commons, Selwyn Lloyd. Tradition has it that the Speaker should stand unopposed, but my father and the Liberal Party believed that this was undemocratic and deprived the constituents of their right to vote. I had followed the events avidly, reading the newspapers which were available for us to look at during break in what was known as the Lower Hall. My friends were interested in it too. No one else's father seemed to be standing for Parliament in my immediate circle. In her daily letters my mother would include cuttings from the local newspapers and copies of the leaflets that had been sent to voters with my father's picture on the front.

At the time, the Liberal Party was undergoing something of a revival under the charismatic leadership of Jeremy Thorpe. He was good-looking and was a more appealing personality than either Edward Heath or Harold Wilson. He had a good rapport with the press who followed his every move. In the days when hardly anyone ever travelled in a helicopter, Jeremy would arrive in one to help a local candidate and do a walkabout followed by television cameras. It is said that Edward Heath, then the leader of the Conservative Party, offered Thorpe the post of Home Secretary after the February 1974 election resulted in a hung Parliament. In retrospect, it was a tactical error for him to have turned this down.

My father's showing in the polls was not particularly notable in the 1974 elections. The Wirral was, after all, one of the safest Tory seats in the country. However, my father was thought to be a good candidate who had argued the case for opposing the Speaker well and so was the natural choice when a by-election was called in 1976 as a result of Selwyn Lloyd's death.

The Liberals generally do very well in by-elections, although results are better when the Tories are in power. Labour were in government in 1976, so the Liberals were not particularly hopeful about winning a safe Tory seat like the Wirral. There was due to be another by-election on the same day in Carshalton in Surrey which did not look very promising either. None the less, my father was given the resources to put up a hard fight. The glare of the media was on us.

All the public meetings were extremely well attended. My father was an excellent public speaker, but early in the campaign he found the attention of the national press and the larger audiences slightly daunting. One evening, we went to the house of a party worker before the meeting and, just as we were about to leave, my father was handed a glass of brandy. My father, who had never drunk much, took it.

'Why are you drinking that?' I asked.

'Dutch courage!' he replied. It had not occurred to me that he might be nervous. He seemed so self-assured when he stood up to speak. I have always been a great admirer of my father's abilities and it was the first time I saw that he was vulnerable to nerves like anyone else.

Because the constituency was large, my father and his campaign manager decided to split it into five distinct areas, each with its own headquarters. There were many empty shops around at the time and the landlords were happy to grant six-week leases and get a bit of income on their underperforming assets. They acted as an information-gathering point for canvassers and election addresses and leaflets were stacked everywhere. The Liberal Party has always been well organized at the grass-roots level and coachloads of canvassers arrived each weekend from other constituencies. Even during the week, there were many outside visitors offering help.

I was no stranger to political campaigning. My father had been a local councillor and had also been in charge of the 'Keep Britain in Europe' campaign in the North West in 1975. I found politics very exciting and even thought that I might want to be a politician one day. Although I was only fifteen when the by-election happened, I went canvassing almost every day. I was about to do my O levels and should have been studying hard, but I was determined to do as much as I could to help. My parents always took a relaxed attitude to my academic work, assuming that I would get through exams without working night and day. I had missed the two election campaigns of 1974 and relished the prospect of playing a more active role this time.

Few people seemed to think that it was odd being canvassed by a teenage girl. All the parties had young activists involved in their campaigns and some people recognized me as the Liberal candidate's daughter from photographs in the local newspaper. When I knocked on the door of one house, the man who answered it took one look at the huge orange rosette pinned to my jumper and said, 'No good asking me to vote for you bloody Liberals. I'm an anarchist.'

'What do you mean you're an anarchist?' I asked.

'I mean I don't agree with anyone,' he said.

'Does that make you an anarchist?' I asked. 'I mean, do you believe in the rule of law? Do you think that the police have a right to enforce law and order?'

'Of course I do,' he said.

'Well, you can't be an anarchist then,' I said.

'I'm not talking to a smart-arse like you!' he said and slammed the door in my face. As far as I was concerned, he was the smart-arse. Being an anarchist was a ridiculous notion. I pulled myself together and went on to the next house.

The next day, I was canvassing in the same area and knocked on another door. A pleasant lady opened it and nodded as I explained why I was there. She edged out of the door, pulled it to and leaned towards me, whispering in confidential tones, 'I'm going to vote for you, dear, but I don't want my husband to know. He votes Conservative and he wouldn't like it if he knew I wasn't going to do the same.' A shout came from inside.

'Who are you talking to, Doreen?'

She pushed the door open again and started talking to me very loudly, 'Well, thank you for telling me all about the Liberal Party and I'm sorry I can't help.' The door shut.

I was very upset by this glimpse into that poor woman's life, chained like a slave to that awful man and not even allowed to think for herself. Still, he could not go into the polling booth with her and I smiled at the thought of her putting her 'X' against my father's name in defiance of him. I had been brought up in an environment where my father regarded my mother as his equal and where I had been given all the same opportunities as my brother. It was a shock to realize that other women were not as lucky.

On the whole, I was amazed by the widespread ignorance and lack of interest in politics. Many did not know who the Prime Minister was or who their MP had been and most had no idea who the by-election candidates were. There was, however, one politician who seemed to be universally known and popular: Jeremy Thorpe.

'Will he be coming here?' I was frequently asked. 'Be sure to bring him round here if he does, won't you dear.' I marked each response on my copy of the electoral register as I went.

The intensity of our campaign was beginning to have some effect. One day, as I was stuffing envelopes in one of the campaign headquarters, I heard an item on the local radio news saying that a new poll showed the Liberals up from 12 per cent at the General Election to 25 per cent and gaining ground rapidly. Our cause had already been helped by frequent visits from members of the parliamentary party including Clement Freud, Cyril Smith and David Steel. There were only thirteen Liberal MPs, but they were all well-known personalities. Jeremy Thorpe's eagerly awaited visit was still to come. That, we thought, would be our trump card.

Victory was still unlikely, but Labour could be pushed into third place and that in itself would be an outstanding achievement. Press comment was very favourable. I used to go through all the newspapers every morning and cut out any relevant articles. The *Financial Times* described my father as 'tweedy and tousled, but easily the best candidate'. The Tory candidate, David Hunt, went on to become a cabinet minister, so the *FT*'s comment was praise indeed. My father's agent was becoming more confident by the day.

Then disaster struck. Jeremy Thorpe, our popular and charismatic leader, was implicated in a bizarre scandal. The details were unclear at first, but it centred on allegations made by an unsavoury character called Norman Scott. Homosexuality was implied, but the newspapers hesitated to say so outright. Shortly after the news broke, the Prime Minister, Harold Wilson, stood up in the House of Commons and talked of a suspected plot by the South Africans to discredit the Liberal Party.

Immediately the scandal broke, a senior local police officer came round to inform my father that, for our own safety, a Special Branch officer would be stationed permanently outside our house. This seemed to have more to do with Harold Wilson's fears that the Liberal Party was being infiltrated than with any direct threat to us. Because it all sounded so bizarre, it was difficult to feel really afraid. What could possibly happen to us? None the less, it was comforting to know that the police were taking it so seriously.

The press arrived en masse, sat outside our gates and followed us wherever we went. I used to go to school on the bus, but the day after the scandal erupted, I was convinced that I was being followed. I managed to lose the tabloid reporter as I disappeared into a sea of uniformed girls when I got off the bus. My mother was furious and decided that she would drive me to school each day until all the fuss subsided. But the tabloids wanted a story and they were determined to get it. As we pulled away one day, a journalist from the *Daily Express* ran up to the car and asked if my mother had anything to say. Other journalists clustered round, anxious not to miss out. She rolled down the window. 'Yes, there is something I would like to tell you. My tom-cat has been neutered,' said my mother in a calm, quiet voice. Then she sped away, leaving the journalists open-mouthed. We both burst into fits of laughter.

The day of Jeremy Thorpe's visit arrived. We had been looking forward to it so much, but now we were dreading it. Jeremy was determined to help us, although, in retrospect, it probably would have been better if he had kept away. My mother and I were given the task of looking after him while my father drove ahead of us in the loudspeaker car, announcing his arrival. On the way to the first walk-about destination, Jeremy asked my mother if she could stop at an off-licence and get him a bottle of whisky. By the end of the day, he had drunk two-thirds of it. Perhaps the alcohol numbed his intense emotional stress, but it also induced a state of melancholy. At one point he told us that, if it had not been for his son, to whom he was devoted, he would have committed suicide. To see someone who usually had such energy and exuberance so deeply depressed was heartbreaking and my mother and I were very concerned about his state of mind.

It was a tense moment for us when he got out of the car for the first walkabout. We could not imagine how this sad creature could go and meet the public and we worried about what the reaction might be. But Jeremy's enormous popularity was still evident and people flocked towards us the moment they saw him. A complete change came over him. He shook hands, exchanged jokes, kissed the odd baby. He betrayed not a hint of the turmoil inside. I was really impressed with his ability to put on a show for the audience, to behave as if he were still riding the crest of the wave and, at least for that moment, make people believe it. Later in life, I was to experience a trauma that put me at the centre of the media's attention. It was nothing on the scale of what Jeremy Thorpe endured, but having had that experience, I am even more amazed by how he managed to cope.

The scandal did not deter the parliamentary party and the activists who redoubled their efforts in the face of this new danger. A public meeting was held, attended by the whole parliamentary party except Jeremy, and my father made the best speech I have ever heard him make. The packed audience clapped and cheered. I thought that there was some hope. Perhaps the voters would look at my father as an individual and recognize that he was the best candidate. I soon realized, however, that scandals like that are impossible to shrug off. The precise nature of what Jeremy was being accused of was difficult even for us to understand, but there was a lot of bad press and even those who still admired him felt less inclined to vote Liberal. The big question now was whether my father would get the 5 per cent of the vote he needed to retain his deposit. To go from an almost certain second-place finish to losing his deposit was a horrifying prospect.

On the day of the by-election, I was allowed to take the

day off school and we all worked really hard right up to the moment the polling stations closed. We spent the first half of the day taking down the numbers on people's polling cards at the polling stations so that we could see which of our known supporters had voted and which had not. In the late afternoon, we started the 'knocking up' process, going to the houses of people who had said they were going to vote Liberal but had not yet voted and urging them to go to the polling station. We could tell that the vote was not holding up well. Many people said that, although they had been going to vote Liberal, the Jeremy Thorpe scandal had changed their minds.

My mother and father went to the count and I spent the evening with our next-door neighbours, eyes glued to the television screen. My parents knew how upset I was about all that had happened and that it would be difficult for me not to show it, so they thought it better that I did not go with them. The result came through at about midnight. My father got less than 5 per cent of the vote. He had lost his deposit. My eyes filled with tears and I cried and cried. It was so unfair. Events had been completely beyond his control. He had worked really hard and he would have made a fantastic MP. Even as a parliamentary candidate, he had dealt with prospective constituents' problems effectively and had explained complicated issues to them clearly. My father looked tired and drawn as the numbers were read out.

If it had not been for the scandal, my father would have come second. The senior members of the Liberal Party thought that he had handled a difficult situation well and, if he had wanted to fight another by-election, he would have stood a good chance of being selected as a candidate, perhaps in a more marginal constituency. He might even have eventually made it to the House of Commons. But the horrors of what we had been through with the scandal, the Special Branch and my father losing his deposit led my mother to beg him to give up politics. He agreed that he would not stand for Parliament again, although he did stay on the party's National Executive.

My friends at school had been very supportive of my father's campaign. They had come to public meetings with me and some of them had even persuaded their parents to put up posters in their front gardens. When I walked through the school gates on the day after my father's terrible defeat, I was really nervous. I did not know whether I would be teased, ignored or made fun of – all sorts of horrible scenarios were going through my mind. But they were very kind to me and everybody agreed that it was just bad luck. I knew then that these were real friends. They were prepared to stick by me in adversity.

My O level results did not suffer from the time I spent campaigning. For my A levels, I chose to do Maths, Further Maths and History. It was an unusual combination and I was the only person doing it, but it fitted with the timetable so it was deemed to be acceptable. I had been going to do Latin, Greek and History, but changed my mind at the last minute because I was bored with Classics. I have never had to try at Maths so it seemed like an easy option.

A few months before the exams, I woke up with a very swollen neck and a rash all over my hands and feet. The blood test showed that I had glandular fever and it was the worst illness that I have ever had in my life. I lost about two stone in weight and had to stay at home for two months. My friends sent me copies of their classwork so that I could try to keep up, but I could not help falling behind. I was a year younger than the rest of my class, so postponing the exams for a year seemed like a reasonable option. But I hated this idea. I had been building up to the exams and I wanted to get them over and done with. Besides, staying at school for another year after my friends had left would be unbearable.

Whilst I was waiting for my results, I annoyed my mother constantly by saying that I had done really badly. I am not sure that I really believed this, but I had no clear sense of how I had done. It had always been assumed that I would be taking the Oxbridge exam, but I kept telling my mother that she would have to accept that I might not be going to university at all. I am usually an optimist, but on this occasion I thought that if I was prepared for the worst, any surprise could only be good. The A level results were pinned to a board at school one day in the summer holidays, so my mother drove me to the gates and waited while I went in to see what I had got. I ran back to the car and my mother could tell from the broad grin on my face that it was good news. My place at Bristol University was secure and my grades were good enough to apply to Oxford or Cambridge.

I deferred my place at Bristol for a year and stayed on at school for an extra term to take the Oxbridge exam in November. Whether I got a place or not, I would have almost a year off before going to university the following September. I had all sorts of ideas about travelling in India or South America, but my parents were not keen on the idea of a seventeen-year-old girl travelling so far afield. I was not particularly eager to go either, so I gave in easily when they objected.

When he was my age, my father had won an English-Speaking Union exchange scholarship to a school in New Jersey called Lawrenceville. He had had a wonderful time and he suggested that I should apply. The glamour of foreign lands was lacking since they speak the same language in the US and I was also slightly put off by the idea of going back to school when I had just left. Still, it seemed like the best option available.

I won the scholarship and the English-Speaking Union decided that I would go to the Phillips Exeter Academy in New Hampshire with one other scholar, Nick Mirsky. We left on a cold February morning, rather bizarrely on an Air India flight. I had never been to the US before and I had not been on a Jumbo either. I was extremely excited and not in the least daunted by the prospect of not seeing my family for several months. When we arrived in Boston, it was bitterly cold and there was snow on the ground.

Nick and I had expected Exeter to be broadly similar to a British boarding school, so we were astonished by what we found. The campus was like a small university. There was an enormous library which had been designed by a famous architect and was on the list of distinguished buildings for architectural students and foreign architects visiting the US. There were about thirty tennis courts, two ice-hockey rinks, an indoor track, an outdoor track, two Olympic-sized swimming pools, endless football pitches, twenty squash courts, an art gallery, two theatres, a music building, a well-stocked bookshop and several restaurants. We had been used to the most basic facilities at our schools in the UK and we could not believe the contrast.

Exeter had originally been a boys' school, but had begun to take girls a few years previously. When we arrived, the ratio was nearly fifty-fifty. I stayed in a small New England wooden house with six other girls. One of the English teachers and his wife lived there with us and were responsible for our pastoral care. They would regularly invite us all into their rooms for a drink and a chat and they showed great interest in us all as individuals. I keep in touch with them to this day. The other girls were all very different. Two were very streetwise and into drugs and I found it difficult to relate to them. Two more were very bookish and, although we did not have a great deal in common, they were very kind to me and helped me find my way around when I first arrived. One was completely star struck and wanted to be a movie star; I thought she was great fun. The sixth, Debby Stalker, was just like me.

Debby and I were both interested in the theatre and writing and wanted to travel. We instantly became friends and agreed that, after graduation, she would come with me to England and we would travel round Europe by train. My parents, relieved that I had given up ideas of India and South America, agreed to this plan on the condition that we found a couple of boys to accompany us.

At Exeter, I had suddenly found a group of people who,

like me, believed that you should pack as much as you could into each day. The extensive facilities ensured that you never had a quiet moment. I spent half my time in the theatre and the other half in the music building. I participated in two dramatic productions in my five months at Exeter and took part in several concerts as part of the choir. All students had to take four subjects, one of which had to be American History. The other three subjects that I chose were Drama, Playwrighting and Art History. I had taken my A levels and Oxbridge exam so there was no point in doing Maths or English. I was there to enjoy myself.

The atmosphere could not have been more different from the English girls' boarding school culture that I was used to. The girls were allowed to do exactly what the boys did and, like university students, we could wander backwards and forwards to the town when we felt like it. We did not have to account for where we were for every minute in every day. Because the adults trusted us and treated us as individuals capable of thinking for ourselves, we felt a sense of responsibility to them. As well as everything else, Exeter taught us to stand on our own two feet. If it was not so difficult to move between the two educational systems, I would send my own children there.

three

How many people actually end up being what they say they want to be when they are children? I had a friend at school who said from the age of five that he was going to work for British Rail. His loft at the family home was covered with yards and yards of track and perfect replicas of steam trains raced around it, going through tunnels and junctions before finally drawing to a stop at one of the three stations. Many years later, my father was stuck at Doncaster Station and, as he waited, he glanced at the posters that lined the platform. One was a notice giving details of Easter train services in the region. At the bottom of the notice was my friend's name.

I was not sure what I wanted to be until I was eight years old. We were driving down to London from Cheshire to see my grandmother. I vividly remember my father suddenly asking as we approached Lord's Cricket Ground, 'Do you know what you want to be when you grow up, Nic?'

I thought for a moment and then answered firmly, 'I want to be an actress.'

From that day on, I was determined that I would indeed

be an actress. Because there were so few girls at Kingsmead, I had had a role in every school production and this had given me a taste for the theatre. I had drama lessons at Cheltenham and Birkenhead, took part in and directed school plays and entered all the local speech and drama competitions and festivals. At sixteen, I applied to the National Youth Theatre and was invited to an audition in Manchester. Two of my friends from Birkenhead High had applied, but I was the only one who got through to the final audition.

As my mother drove me to the audition, I was feeling very nervous and was going over the lines of my two pieces in my head. Two miles outside Manchester, a car smashed into the back of us. We were stationary at traffic lights when it happened and the force of the impact shunted us into the path of the oncoming traffic. We both suffered from shock, although our car was not badly damaged. I was forty-five minutes late and my mother asked if the audition could be postponed, but we were out of luck. As we waited outside the door of the audition room I felt desperate, unable to remember any of the words. When I got into the room, I was still feeling for them, stumbling occasionally and searching the recesses of my mind. The audition was lousy. Needless to say, I did not get a place in the National Youth Theatre company. I was absolutely devastated.

My lack of success did not put me off, because I knew that without the crash I would have done much better. My confidence was given a boost when a friend and I entered the Crosby Festival, the biggest speech and drama competition in North West England, with a piece from *Gigi*. I was playing Gigi and in the final lines of the scene, I had to fall over and the curtain was meant to come down. I managed to fall too far forward and, in order to avoid the curtain falling across my middle, I had to lift my legs up in the air which caused great hilarity in the audience. The piece was meant to be amusing, but it was certainly not a farce. Despite this slight hitch, we won the drama cup and we were overcome with excitement.

The next year, just before I was due to take my A levels, I applied to RADA. I thought it was pretty unlikely that I would get an audition but it was worth a try. I imagined that most of the people applying would already have done some professional or semi-professional work as children and at least would have been to stage school. To my amazement, I was invited to an audition. As for the National Youth Theatre audition, I was asked to prepare a piece of Shakespeare and an extract from a modern play. I chose one of Hermia's speeches from *A Midsummer Night's Dream* and a speech from Tennessee Williams's *The Glass Menagerie*. This required a Southern drawl and I was determined to get the accent right. I knew it would be difficult, but I liked the piece. There were no Americans living anywhere near us in Cheshire, so I rang up the American School in London and asked if I could come and talk to a pupil with a Southern accent. I went to the school armed with a tape recorder and a girl willingly read the speech for me. I spent hours listening to the tape and trying to say the words in exactly the same way.

On the day of the audition, I went down to London by myself on the train. Two people were present in the room.

Apart from greeting me and asking me to start, they said nothing else. I felt more nervous than I had ever felt in my entire life, but I did not forget the words or the accent. At the drama festival, I had found the presence of a large audience much easier to play to. Being in a room with two people who seemed completely uninterested in me made me extremely self-conscious. I could not help thinking that if they thought I was any good, there would be a glimmer of an expression on one of their faces. It was almost as if I was standing in the room by myself and I found it difficult to feel any real passion. When I had done both pieces, they thanked me and I was dispatched to another room to wait.

The next stage was an interview with the deputy principal. He was much more jolly. He clasped my hand and said how delighted he was to meet me. I felt immediately at ease. He sat at his desk and looked at me quizzically.

'Why do you want to come here now? You are a clever girl. Why don't you go to Oxford or Cambridge, participate in all the drama that goes on there and then come back and audition?'

He said that he thought that I had some talent, but that I was too young at seventeen to come to RADA. Over the years, they had taken many people after they finished at university and the standard of drama was very high at most of them. I was disappointed, but I knew he was right. Going to university gave me more options for the future. As I sat on the train on the way back to Cheshire, I wondered if he had meant it when he said that I had some talent or whether he was just trying to humour me. I would not have got a final audition for the National Youth Theatre or won the Crosby Festival if I had no talent. No, he had shown a spirit of paternalism and so I took his advice and applied to Oxford.

My parents had often taken me to Oxford when we went to visit my brother at Stowe and I had already begun to dream of going to university there. But knowing that I wanted to go to Oxford was not enough. The university is made up of individual colleges and it is the college rather than the university that offers you a place. People select their preferred college for all sorts of reasons: other family members who went there, a school affiliation, a geographical connection (Jesus College is largely Welsh) or a particular admissions policy (Hertford College was amongst the first specifically to target comprehensive schools). Prior to 1979, your choice was limited if you were female. There were five colleges which were female and a small number of others which were mixed. Most of the others were all male. In 1979, that all changed. The majority of men's colleges in Oxford and Cambridge opened their doors to women and some of the women's colleges welcomed men.

It still amazes me that this change occurred so recently. It came at a time when equal opportunity in the workplace was a hot issue and I suppose that Oxford and Cambridge had to accept that they could not go on favouring men over women. I am certain that this discrimination is largely to blame for the relatively small number of women in positions of real power today, but the fact that many more women received an Oxbridge education during the eighties means that this will change. I have no doubt that an increasing number will emerge at the top in the next few years.

In 1978, the year I sat my A levels, I knew virtually nothing about Oxford colleges, but Balliol was a college that was mentioned in Evelyn Waugh's novels and I knew that many famous politicians had been there. My father's parliamentary campaign had whetted my interest in politics. I knew that Balliol leaned to the left politically: I could never have gone to a college that was right wing. I was sure that Balliol was the college I wanted to go to. That year, for the first time, women were allowed to apply.

Miss Kellett, my headmistress, was delighted that I wanted to do the Oxbridge exam and confident that I would get a place, but she suggested that we should consider other possibilities before I made a final decision. 'Balliol is a very tough college to get into,' she said. She told me that only the strongest candidates applied there. Competition to get in was amongst the stiffest in Oxford and no one knew how the decision to admit women would affect things. I promised her that I would look at some other colleges.

The women's colleges seemed to be particularly good at organizing open days, so I went to see St Hugh's and Lady Margaret Hall. I did not like St Hugh's at all. The students that we met were rather dull and did not inspire me. The grounds at Lady Margaret Hall were fantastic. There were acres and acres of gardens with the River Cherwell running along the side of them. The general atmosphere was better and I decided that, if I did apply to a women's college, it would be Lady Margaret Hall. It was taking in men that year for the first time.

On one of the days that I was in Oxford, I went into the quad at Balliol and sat on a bench. It was spring and there was a beautiful magnolia tree in full bloom outside the dining hall. There was something about the college that really appealed to me. The space was limited compared to Lady Margaret Hall, but I could almost feel the presence of celebrated alumni as I gazed up at the buildings.

As I had gone to the open days, Miss Kellett was prepared to accept that I had given the matter enough thought and allowed me to apply to Balliol. Now I had to decide what subject I was going to do. I did not want to do either Maths or History, which had been my A level subjects and so it was a choice between Law and Politics, Philosophy and Economics (PPE). I already had a place at Bristol University, which was to read Law since they did not offer PPE. I planned to take that up if I failed to get into Oxford. Though PPE was my first choice, our Classics teacher, who doubled as the careers adviser, felt that it looked inconsistent if I was applying to one university for one subject and another for something else. She persuaded me to go for Law.

When I went to Balliol for my interview in December 1978, I stayed in a small room on the third floor of the Victorian block in the first quad. It was bare and Spartan, but it was adequate. I wore a brightly coloured dress, a black Russian fur hat and black patent-leather boots. My interviewers were not going to forget me in a hurry.

There were no questions about what I had achieved at school or why I wanted to do Law. Instead, Paul Davies, an eminent academic lawyer who would be one of my tutors if I got a place, asked me the following:

'There was a man who was going on an expedition in the desert. He had prepared himself well and had plenty of supplies. In particular, he had a large canister of fresh drinking water. The night before he was due to leave, he went to sleep. Another man came in the night and put poison in his water canister. Shortly afterwards, a third man came and poured all the water away. The first man went into the desert and died of thirst. Who was responsible for his death?'

I thought for a while and then began to put forward what I thought were pretty logical arguments for the second man. Paul Davies demolished these with one sentence and Jo Raz, the other tutor who was interviewing me, giggled. I began to get exasperated and I put forward a new set of arguments in support of the first man being the guilty party. Paul refuted them equally adeptly. I was completely confused and left the room feeling humiliated and certain that I had blown it.

I spent a tense few days at home waiting for a response from Balliol. I thought I had failed that horrendous interview. I was haunted by the riddle that I had been given, went over all the possible arguments and thought about who the guilty man must have been. At least I had tried as many lines of thought as I could in the time that had been available to me and, even though I was panicking inside, I did not think that it had been too outwardly apparent. I thought that there was still an outside chance that I would get a place.

Just before Christmas, I heard that I had got in. My parents were over the moon and my father brought home a bottle of champagne to celebrate. There was one other girl in my year at Birkenhead who had applied to Oxford and she had got into Balliol as well. Out of the thirty girls who entered the college in 1979, two were from Birkenhead High School.

Although Balliol had an image of being a left-wing and relatively informal college, this did not mean that the men necessarily welcomed the arrival of women. Many of the male students were clearly opposed to the invasion of their fortress by these frivolous young girls. The more left wing they were in their political views, the less keen they seemed to be on the change. They saw the Junior Common Room as a place where they could discuss political theories until the early hours of the morning. The introduction of women would, in their eyes, be a distraction. It took us about two terms to really gain acceptance in the JCR. I was never an active member, but there were women in my year who were and participated fully in the politics of it.

All new students were entitled to a room in college during the first year and I had the choice of living on a mixed staircase or in a women-only section. I did not like the idea of sharing a bathroom with a whole lot of men, so I chose the latter. My room overlooked the main quad. It was quite small, but very comfortable and it had the advantage of being directly opposite the bathroom. There was no shower fitting on the bath, however, and so I bought one. I left it in the bathroom one day by mistake and it disappeared.

The next time I wanted to wash my hair, I had to go down to the showers which were in the basement. It was early on a Sunday morning and everyone else was asleep. I put my things down and shut the door. I froze. Loud snores were coming from the cubicle opposite. I opened the door again and went over to see who was making the noise and as I looked round the door, I saw a filthy tramp with long, matted grey hair asleep in the empty bath, fully clothed. I was horrified and ran all the way back up three flights of stairs to my room. Some of the Trotskyite elements in the JCR regularly invited tramps into the college and bought them food. It was fine in my eyes to give them food, but I drew the line at letting them sleep in the bathrooms. Now that there were women in the college, they owed it to us to think a little more carefully before encouraging it.

The many years that I had spent at a boys' prep school had been good training for being one of the first women in a men's college and I did not feel intimidated by the men in any way whatsoever. Women were part of college life now and the men were just going to have to accept that. It was ironic that a college that liked to portray itself as being tolerant found it harder than most to cope with the change.

Oxford was dramatically different from school. I realized that we had been spoonfed until that point. There were only one or two tutorials each week. It was compulsory to attend these which we did in pairs. Both students would write an essay and one would read it out in the tutorial and then discuss it whilst the other would hand his or hers in.

During the remainder of the week, there was a full programme of lectures, but it was not an absolute requirement to attend. Most of the textbooks that we had were written by Oxford professors and, particularly in Contract Law, we were very privileged to be able to hear them speak. The two textbooks that we had for this subject were written by Professors Atiyah and Treitel. The books were excellent, but both professors were particularly entertaining in the flesh.

Even allowing for attending lectures and writing one or two essays each week, there was plenty of time to pursue other interests and this suited me as I was keen to do as much as I could whilst I was at Oxford. My five months at Exeter had been good preparation as it had taught me to think for myself a little more than I had had to do at my English schools. Having been away from home before was also a benefit. There were quite a few eighteen-year-olds who had never been more than ten miles away from home and found it difficult to adjust.

I still clung to a vague ambition to be an actress, but I was less sure that this was what I really wanted to do. Every year, there is a drama competition for first-year undergraduates called Cuppers. I decided to enter with some of my new friends at Balliol. We were required to do a whole play and we chose Peter Shaffer's *Black Comedy*. There was a time restriction, so we had to do some imaginative rewriting of the script. The setting is a party in a flat which suffers a power cut. At the beginning, before the power goes off, the actors are in complete darkness behaving as though it is light and then the light comes up and they have to pretend that they are in the dark. We did not win, but the play was popular with the audience.

The following summer, I went to a director's audition at St John's College, who were planning to put on a play in their splendid garden. I had never directed a play before, but I was keen to try and I thought that Alan Ayckbourn's *Round and Round the Garden* would be suitable, especially given that it was a garden production. The committee agreed and I had the job. Finding the cast was more difficult than I had expected. The main character is a shambolic man called Norman and although I held many auditions, I could not find anyone suitable. There was a chap in the year above me at Balliol who was exactly as I imagined Norman to be, but I had no idea whether he could act. Still, I asked him if he would consider it. He was very dismissive of the idea, but eventually he gave in. Much to his surprise, we discovered that he had real acting ability.

As I entered my second year, I decided to set up my own theatre company. There was an awful lot of Shakespeare performed at Oxford, but not much else. I wanted to appeal to a wider audience so, with some friends, I set up the Oxford Contemporary Theatre Company whose main purpose was to perform the work of modern playwrights. Our first production was *The Crucible* by Arthur Miller, which I directed. My first task was to find a venue. I managed to book a Methodist church which was a great bonus as the play is about the Salem witch hunts and has a strong atmosphere of Puritanism.

I had learned a great deal from my acting experiences at Exeter about how to get a large cast to work closely together. Before rehearsals, we would do various exercises which had the dual benefit of encouraging teamwork and breaking down barriers between people who did not know each other very well. At first there was a fair degree of resistance to this approach, which I put down to the inhibitions of the English. After a week or so, however, the cast could see that the exercises were helpful and they began to participate in them with enthusiasm.

Many of the main parts were played by people I had already met in other productions, including my new discovery, but some of the actors were unknown to me. Although she had auditioned well, I was beginning to have doubts about the actress playing Elizabeth Procter. The problem was made worse by the fact that we had a very strong actor playing John Procter and the scenes which involved them both did not work at all. I arranged extra rehearsal time for her on her own, but I still could not get her to perform with real passion. As the first night approached she did not improve. In the end, I had to tell her that I did not want her in the production. It was a difficult decision, but I felt that I owed it to the rest of the cast as I thought that it would ruin the whole thing if I allowed her to go on stage. She was absolutely furious and stormed out of the room. Where was I going to find another Elizabeth Procter at such short notice? I had spent so much extra time rehearsing the part with her that I knew it off by heart. The obvious thing to do was to play it myself.

During the week of the production, I was under **enormous**

pressure. Although I knew the words pretty well, I had virtually no time to learn them properly as I was making the costumes. My directing role was not over as the dress rehearsal was still to happen. For the first time, I thought I might have taken on too much. On the first night, there was a terrifying moment in the first scene when I forgot my lines, but Jeffrey Gibson, who was playing John Procter, was a very experienced actor and he managed to steer me back on course before the audience noticed. *The Crucible* is such an emotional play that I felt completely drained by the end of the week. My mother came to see the play on the final night and was rather taken aback when I burst into tears over a minor disagreement when we went out for dinner afterwards. Somehow, I had managed to hold it all together but I decided that the next play would have a smaller cast.

We chose *Equus* for our next production. I had a major role, but I asked Jeffrey to direct it. He designed the set which was like a massive roundabout and at various stages the cast who were not performing on it had to turn it round at speed, which added enormously to the drama. I had seen the play at the National Theatre, where the horses had had huge metal feet and metal-framed heads. I wondered whether the National could be persuaded to lend them to me. There was only one way to find out, so I rang the costume department and was amazed when they agreed that I could borrow them. We performed every night for a week and did a Saturday matinée; every show was sold out.

I adored my theatrical experience at Oxford, but by the end of my first year I knew that I did not want to spend the rest of my life as an actress. I wanted a job where there was some certainty. I knew that it was possible that I would be married before too long and I wanted to have children. A job which involved long stays away from home would not be suitable. When I really thought about it, I realized that I am the sort of person who likes to look forward and have some idea of what the future holds. That definitely ruled out being an actress.

I was still drawn to the idea of a career which involved performing and I thought that broadcasting or journalism might be the answer. So, in addition to the plays that I was involved with, I joined the Oxford Broadcasting Society. This was responsible for providing much of the programming for the hospital radio station at the new John Radcliffe Infirmary. It was no more than a poor imitation of Radio 1 initially and the society was trying to think of ways to improve it. I went to a meeting in New College one day and volunteered to interview some famous people. The other members were sceptical about whether I would be able to persuade anyone famous to let me interview them, but they agreed that it would be great if I could.

The society was the proud owner of two professional tape machines, so I took one of them and set off for London the following week. I arrived at Radio 1 in Portland Place without any prior warning and asked if I could interview one of the disc jockeys, fully expecting to be sent away with a flea in my ear. I sat in the lobby waiting to be told to go away but, to my amazement, one of the producers came down to speak to me. I explained that I was a member of the Oxford Broadcasting Society and that we were responsible for several slots on the hospital radio station. I was filled with complete disbelief when I was invited upstairs to interview Dave Lee Travis. He was the most popular of the Radio 1 disc jockeys amongst my generation and I felt extremely honoured to meet him. Because I had been so pessimistic about my chances, I had not prepared anything, so I asked the first question that came into my head.

'Did you imagine, Dave, that you might become a disc jockey when you were a child?' It was a pretty banal question, but it started the ball rolling. The interview was easy after that.

I thought a newsreader would make a good contrast to Dave Lee Travis, so I left the BBC and set off for the headquarters of ITN feeling encouraged but certain that the previous interview had been beginner's luck. Again I was amazed when I was told that Leonard Parkin, one of the presenters of *News at Ten*, would be delighted to give me an interview. Because this was my second interview, I had more of a feel for the sort of questions that I should be asking. I could not wait to get back to Oxford and play the tapes to the President of the Broadcasting Society. She would be as amazed as I was by my success. The one thing that I had learned was that you do not get anything unless you ask.

In the end I did about ten interviews for the Oxford Broadcasting Society. The ultimate coup was persuading Michael Parkinson to come and be interviewed live in Oxford. *The Parkinson Show* was then at the peak of its success and he was one of the most popular television personalities in Britain. I was the President of the Law Society and it was in this capacity that I invited him, but he agreed that we could record the interview and broadcast it on hospital radio. The only venue big enough to hold the audience that I expected the event to attract was the Oxford Union. I went to see my friend William Hague (now leader of the Conservative Party) who was then President of the Union. William was one of the foremost political figures in our year, having made his name by making a speech at the Conservative Party Conference when he was only sixteen years old. When he stood for the presidency of the Union, he was elected with a large majority. What I liked about him was that he was completely straightforward and unpretentious. I suggested that we should make the Parkinson interview a joint event between the Law Society and the Union. William was pleased to have something different to add to his programme of events and readily agreed.

William and I decided that we would take our guest to the Sorbonne (one of Oxford's finest restaurants at the time) before the interview. I was racked with nerves and could hardly eat, but Michael Parkinson was a sweety and put me completely at ease. He talked to us as his equals and was not at all stuffy. William and I asked him about his career and he was full of fascinating anecdotes. By the end of the meal, I still had a tinge of nerves, but I was actually looking forward to the interview. I had done my research into his life and career very thoroughly and a clipboard with my questions was waiting at the Union on my chair.

As we walked into the Union chamber, it erupted with cheers and applause. I took my time, arranging myself in my chair and glancing at my notes. William said a few words of welcome. I drew breath and then looked Michael Parkinson directly in the eye as I delivered my first question. He grinned from ear to ear and said, 'You've got a nice pair of legs!' I turned bright red and looked down. I had not chosen the best dress to wear. It did up with two buttons on the waistband and consequently, as I sat down, it had opened up revealing most of my right leg. In my nervous state, I had not even noticed. There were sniggers and giggles from the audience as I desperately rearranged my dress.

The remainder of the evening was fine. Michael was such an accomplished talker that I just had to ask one short question and he would take five minutes to reply.

'Michael Parkinson, thank you,' I said and the under-graduates burst into more uproarious applause. Performing in plays had prepared me for this event, but it was different because, when I was acting, I could hide behind another persona. That night, I sat in front of a huge audience as me and I enjoyed it thoroughly.

What I loved most about Oxford was that it was possible to do so many different things and fill every minute with some kind of activity. As if I did not have enough to do, I decided to set up a luncheon club called the Oxford Forum. There were a large number of dining clubs, but no lunch-eon clubs. I thought that it would be easier to attract well-known public figures to a lunch as it would mean that they would not have the expense and inconvenience of staying overnight. I thought that this would tie in well with my Broadcasting Society work. Many of my guests were happy to be interviewed for hospital radio as well as doing the lunch.

I wrote to Iris Murdoch and asked if she would be the Honorary President and she agreed. A friend who helped me with the Oxford Forum, Noel Sloan, and I decided that we would have an annual dinner each year and we invited A.L. Rowse, a famous historian, to speak at the first one. Noel and I had both enjoyed reading his books when we were doing our History A levels. Everything went very well until Mr Rowse began to make his speech. Somehow he wandered on to the subject of population control in India and put forward the argument that the West should send 'bushels of contraceptive pills' instead of food and medicines and that if that did not work, then there should be compulsory sterilization after people had had two children. I took exception to this tirade and left the room, leaving Noel to handle the rest of the evening alone. A couple of other girls followed me.

The only other event of the Oxford Forum that was controversial was when John Cory came to speak at one of our lunches. He had put forward a private member's bill which would result in the maximum limit on abortion being reduced from twenty-eight weeks to twenty-four weeks. The subject had become a hot topic of conversation in Oxford and it was a real coup when he agreed to come. There were a number of feminist groups who strongly objected to his position, claiming that it interfered with a woman's right to make her own choice. Some of these women heard that John Cory was coming to a lunch at Balliol and were standing outside the front gate with banners. They were relatively peaceful and did not attempt to come into the college. When John Cory visited the Oxford Union at a later date, there was a full-scale demonstration with many more people, so we got off lightly.

As part of my duties as President of the Law Society, I had to organize a sherry party for incoming freshmen which was held at the Oxford Union. In another room, a similar event was being held by the Cocktail Society. As I was going to the kitchen for more ice, an undergraduate called Tim Horlick spied me from afar and came over to talk to me. He had been at the Cocktail Society party, but he soon became part of ours. Although I am only a couple of months older than Tim, I was in the year above him. I had met him twice before. A few days after he arrived in Oxford, I was walking down Turl Street with a fellow law student called Andrew Cullum when he stopped to greet this tall, dark, and I have to say, handsome young man who was introduced to me as an old school friend of his.

'How are you enjoying Oxford?' I asked. This was an attempt at polite conversation on my part, but Tim thought I was extremely condescending and did not take to me at all.

About ten days later, Andrew was having a tea party for Tim and another of his school friends and asked if I would make him a cake. I was living in a very luxurious flat in Headington which had an enormous and well-equipped kitchen. I arrived slightly late with the cake and Tim came into the room just as I was leaving.

'Was it something I said?' Tim asked.

'I'm not invited. I just made the cake,' I replied.

'Andrew, that's outrageous!'

'She can stay if she wants,' Andrew said, looking rather red in the face, but I didn't mind at all. I had not expected to stay and had lots of things to do, so I left.

That evening at the Union, Tim decided that I was not as bad as he had first thought and, shortly afterwards, a relationship began between us. Most of my previous boyfriends had been easy to push around and had done whatever I had told them, but this was not the case with Tim. He was as strong willed as I was and we both had to learn to compromise. He still says that I always get my own way whereas I maintain that he does.

We had only known each other for a short time but I had a strong feeling that Tim and I were going to be spending the rest of our lives together. As I began to think about my future career, I came to the conclusion that I wanted a job that would keep me in London, which was where Tim planned to be. As my degree subject was Law, I spent some time thinking about whether I wanted to pursue a legal career. I decided the best thing to do would be to get a holiday job in a firm of solicitors in Liverpool, the nearest major city to where my family lived. I was determined to do this off my own bat rather than getting my father to pull strings for me. I wrote several letters and got refusals until finally one firm asked me to come and meet them.

'You must be Michael Gayford's daughter,' said the senior partner as I walked into his office. I felt deeply upset. It was clear that he had agreed to see me because he knew my father rather than on the basis of the CV that I had sent him. Still, now that I was in his office, there was no point in dwelling on this. He offered to employ me for a few weeks and pay me £20 per week plus train fares which was an unexpected bonus. Although it had not been the personal success that I had wanted, I had achieved my aim.

I had worked for my father in the holidays a few times, so the concept of doing an office job was not new to me, but the work I was given was. Much of what I did was fairly monotonous, but I was allowed to accompany one of the partners to an industrial tribunal which was fascinating. At the end of my time with the firm, I had decided that I did not want to be a solicitor. I am a doer and I did not think that I would be very good at giving advice to other people. I would be frustrated if they did not take it and I was not sure that I would get a real sense of achievement even if they did.

That left the possibility of a career at the Bar. One day I went to the law courts in London to see some barristers in action. There was a civil case in the High Court and only two other members of the public were present. A whole morning was spent discussing a complex legal question which went totally over my head. Neither of the barristers was particularly impressive. They were both quietly spoken and made no effort to make the matter seem interesting. I had obviously been watching too many American court-room dramas on television and, in comparison, I found the proceedings pedestrian and boring. Still, I was sure that I had not picked the best case to watch and I did like the idea of wearing a wig and 'performing' in court. The thing that finally put me off was the knowledge that if I did go to the Bar, I would be poverty stricken for years to come.

I had loved my broadcasting experiences so much that I decided to apply for a place on the journalism course at the University of Cardiff. I remember driving down the M4 in my pink mini in a terrific thuderstorm, arriving in Cardiff and being asked to take a general knowledge test along with fifty other people in a room. A few days later, I received an offer of a place.

My father was very against me becoming a journalist. He thought that, rather than writing about what other people were doing, I was the sort of person who would do better in a commercial enterprise. He suggested that I should work for him and then get a job in the City and, if I still wanted to write, I could become a financial journalist which was a rapidly expanding area. I was not sure about the City, but I had enjoyed my holiday jobs with my father, so I agreed. I did not want to give up my Cardiff place entirely and they allowed me to defer it for a year.

My mother was delighted that I would be living at home after three years away at university. My brother was at the Royal College of Music in London and so she was pleased to have one of her children at home for a while before we both finally left to make our own way in life. She thought that working for the firm was an excellent idea. After months of uncertainty about what I was going to do and where I was going to live, I felt positive about the future and was determined to make a success of it.

Roy Wilson, Dickson would not be my first commercial

experience. In my second year at university, a friend called Guy Hands asked me if I wanted to sell pictures for a business that he had established. He had commissioned an artist to produce a number of black and white prints which were then hand-coloured and sold by teams of under-graduates door-to-door in nearby towns such as Aylesbury and Maidenhead. At first I was sceptical and I did not particularly need the money, but I was impressed by his entrepreneurial skills and intrigued to see how the business operated.

The first time that I went out with one of the teams, I did not sell a single picture and I was ready to give up. Guy persuaded me to persevere. I thought hard about what I should say to get the interest of the customers and worked out a patter for myself. I knew that most people liked to feel that they were getting a bargain, but I was working under strict instructions and was not allowed to reduce the prices. Instead, I added £10 to the initial price and then reduced it when I could see that the customer was almost on the hook. I sold two pictures that night. Only the best salespeople made two sales in a night and I was surprised that my simple technique worked so well. I found immense excitement and satisfaction in closing each deal.

I did not have time to go out with Guy's sales teams very often, but when another friend called Nick Bruce suggested that I should work with him in London the following summer, I looked at the idea seriously. Nick was at Balliol with me. He and an old school friend had answered an advertisement in the *Evening Standard* which had been placed by a Watford company that sold coal-effect gas fires.

Half the houses in central London have them now, but this was when they had only just come on to the market. The company was run by a married couple and they were looking for two salesmen and someone to man their display caravan. The idea was that Nick and Jeremy would be the salesmen and I would be the person in the caravan who would get the 'leads'.

We sold a large number of gas fires over the course of the summer. In retrospect I am surprised that anyone was interested in purchasing a gas fire at that time of year, but I suppose they thought of it as a decorative feature. As the beginning of the new term approached, Nick decided to find out how much the manufacturer was selling the fires for. When he realized that the wholesale price was £50 and we were selling them for £200, he suggested that we should set up a similar business serving the Oxford area.

I thought this was an excellent idea and went to see my bank manager in our village in Cheshire. I explained to him what we wanted to do and, to my surprise, he agreed to lend us the money we needed to get the business off the ground. We called the company Heritage Fires. We had great intentions, but when I returned to Oxford I was so busy that I had no time even to contemplate selling gas fires. Nick spent more time on it, but in the end we wound the company up when the loan was repaid.

Roy Wilson, Dickson had two main areas of activity: chemical merchanting and building products. My father had just won an agency from a Canadian company to sell a binder for animal feed pellets in the UK and he gave me responsibility for making it a success. It was not exactly a glamorous product, but I did not care about that. I was looking forward to the challenge.

I had to arrange for the product to be imported into the UK in containers, find storage facilities and organize haulage to the customers. First of all, however, I needed to get some customers. My father told me to find out if there was a trade association for animal feed manufacturers and get a list of the members. He gave me plenty of tips as to how to get started. I prepared product sheets, had them printed and got samples ready to send to potential customers. At last I was ready to ring the first one. I sat at the telephone with a sheet of paper ready to find out as much about the customer as possible.

My self-confidence was boosted as the buyer on the other end of the telephone was very friendly towards me. Yes, he would be interested in another supplier. Yes, he would like me to send a product sheet and a sample. Yes, he was prepared to say who his current supplier was and how much he was paying. If he thought the sample was good enough and the price was competitive, he would like one pallet of the binder to try. I could not believe how easy the call had been. I proceeded to ring other potential customers. Not all of them were anywhere near as co-operative as the first, but I was making good progress. I followed up each telephone call with a letter, a product sheet and a sample. At first, I concentrated on the smaller animal feed manufacturers and got my father to ring the larger ones like BOCM Silcock (which was then part of Unilever and had about eighteen mills of varying size around the country).

Soon after I began this process, I got my first order. I

was thrilled. Then I realized that I actually had to make sure that the order was fulfilled. I went to the shipping manager in a slight panic and asked him how I should go about organizing the container. He gave me the telephone number of C.P. Ships in the UK and I rang them and asked for a quotation to bring a container into Felixstowe. I arranged to meet them and then explained what I was doing and gave them a forecast of how many containers I was expecting to bring in over the next year. The two men that I met must have been in their late forties and they seemed rather bemused that this girl of twenty-one was planning such an ambitious programme of importing into the UK. They could not really believe it and treated me in a rather patronizing manner. I insisted on paying for lunch, saying that they could pay next time when we were actually doing business. They went away, probably expecting never to see me again and that my first container would be the only container. Their attitude irritated me and I hoped that the next time we met, they would take me more seriously. I was going to make sure that they did.

When the container arrived in Felixstowe about two weeks later, disaster struck. I was rung by the port authority to say that when the customs officers opened the container to check it, the bags had split and there was animal feed binder all over the container. I jumped on a train down to London and then took a train to Felixstowe from Liverpool Street Station. I arrived at the container depot and was horrified when the door of my container was opened. There was binder all over the place, but what was most peculiar was that the material had been delivered in bulk bags rather than in 25 kilo bags on pallets. There had obviously been some sort of misunderstanding between us and the Canadian supplier. The bulk bags were tall and thin and that is why they had fallen over and burst. I could not believe my eyes and I then realized that being in business was not quite as easy as it had seemed. What was I going to say to my customer? I was not looking forward to telling him that he would have to wait for his order.

The conversation with my customer was difficult. He was not very impressed that his order was going to be several weeks late, but he still agreed to take the delivery when it eventually arrived. I got my father to speak to the suppliers and explain what we wanted and they said that the next container would contain forty 1 tonne pallets with 25 kilo bags. My father also asked me to do some research into bulk bags so that we could suggest something more suitable if we did have any customers who wanted them in the future.

After this unfortunate start, things began to run more smoothly. At the end of the first year C.P. Ships were forced to forget their scepticism as we had shipped two hundred 40 tonne containers to various destinations in the UK. The attitude of the two men that I had met at the beginning of the project had totally changed. They now treated me with deference. My father was pleased to see that we had generated £1 million of turnover. It was not a very high-margin product, so the profits were not enormous, but they were more than enough to pay my salary of £6,000. I had learned that service and price were the two most important factors. The product was pretty much the same whoever the customer purchased it from. A couple of pounds less per tonne than the competition was enough to get their interest and if it arrived on time and was in good condition, they would use us again.

During that year, I used to go down to Oxford virtually every weekend in term time to see Tim. He was living in a large flat in North Oxford which belonged to his college. He had a lovely room with enormous windows, but very tatty curtains. I was reasonably adept with a sewing machine beause I had always done the costumes for my plays. I bought some fabric in Laura Ashley and each night when I returned home from work, I would get the machine out and work on Tim's new curtains. When we hung them, the room was transformed and Tim was delighted.

It was now eighteen months since we had started going out with each other and we used to talk about the prospect of marriage from time to time. We both thought that it was highly likely that we would end up being married to each other, but we realized that we were a little young to contemplate it. It would be better to wait until we had both decided what careers we wanted and begun to establish ourselves in them. One weekend when I was in Oxford, we were walking past a small antique jewellery shop and saw a lovely art deco, hexagonal diamond ring. We bought it, just in case, and Tim hid it in his bedroom the next time he returned home.

I was reluctant to leave my father's firm as I loved what I was doing so much, but the time had come for me to move on. Most of my friends had left the area and I did not want to spend the rest of my life in Cheshire. London was where I wanted to live so that I could be near Tim. My place at

Cardiff was still open, but my time at Roy Wilson, Dickson had given me a definite interest in business and I did not want to be a journalist any more. I now agreed with my father that the City was the place to work. I wrote direct to a number of investment banks, stockbrokers and merchant banks and received many invitations to go to interviews.

Tim was applying to many of the same companies, but he also had the major accountancy firms on his list. Still being at Oxford made it much easier for him as most of the big firms visited the university on what was called the 'milk round'. I had to go back and forth to London for all my interviews which was very time-consuming. Tim also had the Careers Library at his disposal which allowed him to do his homework on the various firms before his interviews. I had to rely on him to brief me. Once I got to the interviews, I was treated like any other candidate and it did not seem to matter that I had strayed from the normal path. In fact, my business experience became the focal point of most of my interviews.

As I read through the material I had on the various banks and brokers, I found it extremely difficult to understand what they actually did. The only person I could ask was my father and he was not familiar with the City at all. I read the *Financial Times* each day when I arrived at the office and *The Economist* each week in an effort to pick up enough of the jargon to give a vague impression that I had at least tried to find out something about it. Everyone I knew who was applying to a merchant bank seemed to want to do corporate finance, so I went along to my first interview saying that that was what I wanted to do.

'Do you know what a corporate financier actually does?' said my interviewer, who was about thirty-five, arrogant and seemingly devoid of a sense of humour. I was already feeling very ill at ease.

'Well, no,' I said, 'I thought you would be teaching me that as part of the training programme.' That bank did not offer me a job and I dropped the line about wanting to be a corporate financier at other interviews.

One company was far and away my first choice: Warburgs. I had never heard of it before I applied, but I had gathered from other graduates at interviews that the two best merchant banks were Warburgs and Morgan Grenfell. When I arrived at Warburgs, I was impressed with the interest that was taken in us. At other banks, those waiting to be interviewed had been left in a room unattended. Warburgs laid on a succession of young executives who had been with the bank for two or three years to come and tell us what it was really like working in a merchant bank. This immediately made us relax and when we came to do our four interviews with senior people from each of the four divisions I am sure that we performed better than we would have done otherwise. The whole place had an air of professionalism and, unlike many of the other companies I went to see, they were trying very hard to sell themselves to us. At lunch, David Scholey, the chief executive of the bank, came and said a few words to us. There was a hush when he entered the room; we could tell from his demeanour that he was the boss. Someone whispered in my ear that he used to be one of the backing musicians for Sandie Shaw which I found difficult to believe, but it was true.

Of my four interviews at Warburgs, the most entertaining was with Leonard Licht, a prominent fund manager in the asset management division. He began by saying how gormless most of my fellow interviewees were and he would not give floor space to any of them. I was taken aback by this and had to suppress a giggle. He picked up my application form, pushed it to one side and said, 'I'm not interested in this boring piece of paper. Tell me why I should recommend that you should have a job.'

'Well,' I said, 'I'm ambitious and determined. It sounds to me as though I will get a first-class training at Warburgs and when I have learned what merchant banking is all about, I am prepared to apply myself in my chosen area and help take the business forward.' The words did not really mean anything, but Leonard could tell that I was keen to succeed. For some reason I asked him if he thought it made any difference that I was a woman.

'Absolutely not!' he said emphatically. He was keen, he told me, to have more women in senior positions in the firm. His wife was a barrister and had had to fight hard to progress in another male-dominated profession. Leonard was wildly different from anyone else that I had met in my interviews. We struck up a real rapport and chatted away as though we had known each other for years.

'Oh well,' he said finally, 'I had better talk to another spotty youth now. I'm sure you've been offered other jobs, but this is the best place to work, you know.' I was absolutely certain that he was right.

four

It was April when I was offered a job at Warburgs, but I did not actually start until October. I continued to sell my animal feed binder and spent a happy summer performing *Twelfth Night* in the garden at home with all the proceeds going to the local hospice. I was Feste the Jester or, as one of the guards called me in the dress rehearsal, Fester the Jester.

Tim was due to start work a month before me as a trainee accountant at Price Waterhouse, so we would be moving to London together. We were twenty-two and had already been going out with each other for two years. The question was, should we get married? I did not believe in living together before marriage. This was not on moral or religious grounds, but I just felt that it was too easy to drift along without having made a proper commitment to each other. Tim felt that we were too young to get married and yet it was clear that it would be a great deal more convenient if we were. Put together, our salaries were enough to cover the cost of a mortgage on a small flat. We decided that we would wait until the marriage issue was resolved before buying a flat, but we did have to live somewhere. My grandmother, who lives in Blackheath, was happy to put me up until I found my feet and Tim rented a room in a house with two extremely charming girls. I think they took comfort from the fact that Tim had a long-term girlfriend who seemed to be pretty bossy and would make sure that he did not wreck their house.

On 3 October 1983, I arrived at Warburgs along with twelve other graduates. As one of the leading merchant banks in the UK, it had a strong position in a number of areas in the financial services industry, and had four distinct divisions: corporate finance, banking, international and asset management. Seigmund Warburg, the founder of the bank, was one of the inventors of Eurobonds, and Warburg's remained one of the foremost players in the Eurobond market. It was also regarded as being the leading house in corporate finance, which involves giving advice to companies on structuring their capital and on takeovers and mergers. The asset management business was still seen as the new firm on the block, but it was expanding rapidly. The success of the bank was due to the fact that there was a strong culture and that sub-standard work was not tolerated. We were told that during the two-year training scheme we would spend six months in each division and then we would decide, in consultation with the personnel department, where we wanted to stay permanently. I and five other graduates started in asset management.

The division was located in a different building round the corner from the main Warburg offices in Gresham

Street. It was a sixties horror with poor facilities, but I did not notice the quality of the office space on the day I started. I was too excited by the prospect of learning about something that was completely new. With my new security pass in one hand and a copy of the *Financial Times* in the other, I was introduced to my first boss, a private client manager called Digby Armstrong. Digby had only been with Warburgs for a short time himself, having had a previous career in the army. He was young and enthusiastic and was keen to involve me in every aspect of his work as he saw this as being the best way for me to learn. He took me on a tour of the office and introduced me to the head of the private client department. There was one other graduate in the department: John Richards. He struck me as being a very serious young man, but I warmed to him immediately. As I got to know him better, I realized that he had a highly developed sense of humour and he had me in fits of giggles regularly. I was very surprised when he told me he was married and even more surprised when he said that he had been for eighteen months.

Digby explained to me that each UK fund manager was responsible for researching a sector of the stock market, regardless of whether their clients were private individuals or pension funds. The whole UK team would meet each morning to discuss views on stocks. Digby's sector was insurance and, if a company had made an announcement or had come into the office to see us, he was expected to comment at the morning meeting. The large stockbroking firms had analysts covering every sector and the insurance specialists would come in to see Digby and send him copies of their written work. Some of them had started at stock-broking firms and learned about the insurance industry, others had come from the industry itself. We did not have to pay anything for their input, but it was expected that, if we valued them, we would put a certain amount of business their way when we bought and sold shares.

It was necessary to speak regularly to the brokers, but of much greater importance was to meet with the companies themselves. Most major companies would come in to see us twice each year and I could see that it was vital to be properly prepared for those meetings in order to get the most out of them. If an insurance company was coming in, Digby was expected to write a detailed briefing note, highlighting the major issues facing the company. After the meeting, he was required to write another note summarizing what was said and in addition he had to report on it at the morning meeting which was minuted. There was no way that any fund manager could claim that he had not been informed of what had taken place. Every so often, there would be a reshuffle of sector responsibilities and the idea was that, over a period of time, fund managers would build up a detailed knowledge of the whole market.

Digby's specific responsibility for the insurance sector did not absolve him of the need to know about other stocks. As a fund manager, he was the person who bought and sold all UK shares for his portfolios. He gained his knowledge of other areas by listening to his colleagues, attending the meetings with companies and reading brokers' notes. By following him wherever he went, I soon began to get a broad overview of the stock market. I felt very privileged to be allowed to attend meetings with Britain's top management in the largest companies. I did not say a word at first, but it was not too long before I plucked up courage to ask the occasional question.

I had enjoyed working with Digby enormously, but John and I were keen to gain some experience of the pension fund department within the division. This part of the business was growing fast and appealed to me more than private clients. It seemed to me that some of the private clients regarded their fund manager as someone who they could bounce all their problems off and it seemed preferable to deal with large pension funds who left the fund manager to get on and manage the money. After two months in the asset management division, John and I moved. We were put on a desk with two new recruits, who were more mature than us and were not on the graduate training scheme. One had been in the navy and the other had been at BP. Both had decided to change careers and knew even less about fund management than we did.

I rather objected to the fact that the experienced fund managers sat in one place and those with no experience sat together in another. We were expected to do a number of mundane tasks which included running between the administration department, taking orders to the dealing room and making the tea. I did not mind this as I knew I had to start somewhere. But I did mind that we did not have a Topic screen (Topic is the stock exchange system which tells you what share prices are during market hours) and so we had no way of knowing what was going on in the market. Digby and I had shared a screen and I had been used to flipping through the pages all day. Stephen Zimmerman, who ran the pension fund department, came up to me one day and said, 'What's the price of Marks and Spencer?' Asking graduates questions like this was one of his favourite pastimes.

'As I haven't got a Topic screen, I can't tell you,' I replied.

'Topic screens cost a lot of money, you know. You can always look at someone else's.'

'It's a little difficult to do that when people are sitting at their desks. They might find it annoying if there are four people constantly trying to look at their screens.' He smiled and walked away. The next day, two screens arrived for us to share.

I realized very early on that you need a sponsor in a large organization. No one is particularly interested in you when you first arrive, but the aim should be to do the tasks that you are set so well that someone in a position of influence notices you and takes you under their wing. I had been so impressed by Leonard Licht when he interviewed me that I decided that he was the person I really needed to impress. People talked about him with enormous respect. He was the best fund manager. He was so good that he sat in his own corner with one other fund manager, Tom Charlton. They had an air of aloofness about them which no one else possessed.

When I first arrived in the pension fund department, Leonard took absolutely no notice of me and did not seem to register that I was the young woman he had interviewed the previous April. Just before Christmas, we were sent away on a residential course at the London Business School to learn how to analyse company accounts. When we came back, we were all eager to start writing notes about companies and use our new skills. When Leonard asked a couple of us to write about some stocks that he had in his portfolios one day, I knew that this was a big opportunity for me. I started by reading every newspaper cutting on the company that had been written over the previous two years and then I looked at the brokers' notes. I talked to some analysts in broking houses who covered the stock. Finally, I spent two days meticulously analysing the accounts using the book that we had been given by the London Business School for reference when I got stuck. I read and reread the final draft, searching for typing errors and then got John to read it. When I was happy with it, I presented it to Leonard. It had taken me five days to write the note. I had completed my assignment before the others and Leonard commented on this. The next day, Leonard sent the note back. He had written on it in his large, distinctive writing: 'Excellent note. Well done!' I sat and stared at it with an immense feeling of satisfaction that he had recognized my hard work.

A few days later, Leonard noticed me walking past his desk and asked me to get him something from the stock department. We were on the fourth floor of the building and the stock department was on the ground floor. I had recently been on a tour of the back office and knew exactly whom to ask for the document that Leonard wanted. Within minutes, I was back at his desk. Again, my speed surprised him. I wanted to make sure that, in his eyes, I stood out from the other trainees and that if he ever decided that there was room for a graduate to work with him and Tom, he would pick me.

During these early days in the City, it never occurred to me that I would be at any disadvantage because I was a woman. It helped that the second in command in the pension fund business was a woman too. Her name was Carol Galley. During my first week at Warburgs, Carol was away on holiday. On my second Monday, I went to the morning meeting with Digby. There was one spare seat left at the centre of the table and, a few seconds after everybody else had arrived, Carol swept into the room and sat down. She looked perfect. There was not a hair out of place, her make-up was meticulously done and her nails were beautifully manicured and varnished. Her clothes were highly tailored and looked to me as though they came from Yves Saint Laurent. No one was allowed to comment on a company without being on the receiving end of an incisive question from Carol.

When I joined the pension fund department, I soon realized that Carol was the person who made the place tick. She paid great attention to detail and was a great admirer of Seigmund Warburg's way of doing things. If she did not approve of something, she would say, 'It's not the Warburg style.' No junior member of the team dared to send a note out with typing errors in it. Carol always told us that we should get our peers to glance at our work before we sent it out and we always did. I liked her approach. I thought that it was right that we should have clear parameters to work within and I was sure that at Warburgs I was getting the best possible training.

Tim had to study hard in the evenings for his accountancy exams, whereas I never had to work beyond 6.30 p.m. I would go over to visit him occasionally and read a book whilst he worked, but more often than not he would do some work and then visit me. Three months after I had started at Warburgs, Tim proposed to me. It was New Year's Eve and I was staying with him and his parents in Bath. Tim had arranged to take me to a very good French restaurant called the Beaujolais. The tables were usually close together, but they were even closer together that night as the proprietor had obviously packed in as many people as possible on what must have been one of the busiest nights of the year. There was a middle-aged couple sitting next to us who did not seem to have anything to say to each other and listened to our conversation instead. When we had eaten our pudding, Tim could bear the suspense no longer. He leaned across the table and whispered, 'Will you marry me?' A small box landed in my lap and I took it in my hand and opened it. In it was the lovely art deco diamond ring that we had bought in Oxford the previous April. I had forgotten quite how pretty it was and, grinning at Tim, said that I would adore to marry him and put the ring on my finger.

We were now nearing the end of our first six months at Warburgs and John and I knew that we would be expected to leave the asset management division and go to banking. We had both enjoyed ourselves so much that we did not want to move and we spent many hours talking about how we could persuade Ross Bunce, who was the fund manager in charge of the graduates, that we should stay. Eventually, we plucked up courage and asked him. As we had expected, he said it would be most irregular for us to stay and that it virtually never happened. He could think of one person who had done so, but she had been a special case. He said that he would have to consult with Carol and Stephen and would get back to us. John and I did a bit of gentle lobbying amongst some of the other fund managers and everyone seemed keen for us to stay. The business was growing so fast that they felt that it would be useful to have a couple of extra pairs of hands. Soon we were told that our wish had been granted.

Shortly after this, we were told that we were to leave our building. It had poor systems, ancient telephones and no air-conditioning and so nobody was sad at this news. The whole of Warburgs was to be housed in a brand-new building. When we arrived at work for the first time in our new surroundings, everyone was ecstatic. The meeting rooms on the sixth floor were palatial. Our new desks were twice the size of the old ones and the technology took us into a different era. The asset management division was doing well before the move, but it seemed to get a new lift after it and business boomed.

Each graduate had to spend a couple of months in the marketing team and just after we moved into the new building, my turn came round. Tim and I had decided to get married in June and so I was constantly thinking about the wedding arrangements. We had to decide where to have our wedding list and choose what we wanted on it. I would spend lunch-time going to the West End for wedding dress fittings and to collect satin shoes for me and the bridesmaids. I had forgotten all about the veil and so had to make another trip to purchase one. My mother and I were constantly on the telephone to each other.

I did my work perfectly well, but I was not as obsessive about it as I had been before. It was clear to David Rosier, who was head of the marketing team, that I had little interest in anything else other than the wedding, but he did not seem to mind. The day before I was due to go up to Cheshire to help with the last-minute preparations, Carol and David took me out for a celebratory drink. They produced a bottle of champagne and I did not dare tell them that I did not drink alcohol and so I drank two glasses of it. I had not eaten any lunch that day and when it was time to leave the wine bar, I could barely stand up.

My mother had planned the wedding meticulously. We were married in the church in the next village to ours in Cheshire and the reception was in a marquee on the lawn. We had decided that we would have the ceremony at 5.30 p.m. and then have dinner and dancing afterwards. All our parents' oldest friends were invited and, when added to all of our friends and family, the guest list came to about 350. There was plenty of room in the marquee, but the church was not very large. On the day, this did not matter. There were one or two people standing at the back, but it was wonderful to walk into a packed church.

Music was a prominent feature of our wedding. My brother, Christopher, was still a student at the Royal College of Music and he had arranged for a trumpeter, an organist and a harpist to play during the ceremony. My father and I arrived in the church to the wonderful sound of a Purcell trumpet voluntary. The harpist played during the signing of the register, the sound reverberating around the small church enveloping the congregation. I was very keen to get away from tradition and avoid the usual bridal marches. Christopher and I had spent hours debating what should be played when Tim and I left the church and I suggested an extract from Mussorgsky's *Pictures at an Exhibition*. At first, my brother was rather dismissive, but when he looked at the music, he noticed that it had originally been written for a piano and a trumpet. It was the perfect choice.

Everyone returned to the house after the service and the champagne began to flow. My father made sure that everyone's glasses were kept full throughout and so, by the time we came to the speeches, the guests were all very merry. Tim's twin brother, William, was the best man and he made one of the best speeches that I have ever heard at a wedding. A large proportion of it seemed to centre on my spending habits and how Tim was going to have to work hard to keep me in the style to which I was rapidly becoming accustomed. Tim forgot the punchline of his only joke, but the audience found that much more funny than they would ever have found the joke itself.

A family friend proposed the toast to Tim and me, but my father could not resist saying a few words at the end. He thanked all those who had travelled from abroad for coming and then he did something that I had never seen before at a wedding. He took a five-pound note, tore it in half and then handed one piece to me and one to Tim.

'If you are ever really hard up,' he said, 'then you will

have to be together if you are going to spend your last five pounds.'

Tim and I spent that night in the Grosvenor Hotel in Chester. It was 1 a.m. by the time we arrived and there was hardly anyone about. We had organized a hire car to be dropped off the next day so that we could drive down to London to catch a plane to Barbados where we were going for our honeymoon, but it did not arrive. Tim and I paced up and down outside the hotel. Tim rang to find out what had happened and it turned out that the chap who was delivering it had overslept. We were sympathetic as we had almost done the same ourselves, but it meant that we had an hour less than we had allowed to get to London.

Tim drove very fast on the motorway in order to make up time. We were just getting near to the M6/M1 junction when a police car came up behind us with its lights flashing. Tim was forced to pull in.

'Tell him that we have just got married and we are trying to catch the plane for our honeymoon,' I said. Tim said all of this, but the policeman was having no excuses and so Tim got a ticket. Not only did this waste a lot of time, but then he had to stick to seventy miles per hour for the remainder of the journey. We got to the check-in desk twenty minutes before the plane was due to take off and I was convinced that they would not let us on board. Initially we were told that we would have to sit separately as there were no seats left together. Luckily, however, I had ticked the 'honeymoon' box on the holiday booking form and the girl who was checking us in noticed this on the computer.

'You cannot sit separately if you are on honeymoon,' she said. 'We'll give you a free upgrade to first class.' We could not believe it.

Tim took full advantage of all the free alcohol that was on offer in the first-class cabin. When we arrived in Barbados, a car was there to meet us. It was quite a long drive and Tim fell into an alcoholic slumber as we drove along the coast. It was phenomenally hot and humid and it felt as though a storm was on its way. We were staying at Cobbler's Cove which is still regarded as one of the best hotels in Barbados. We had an enormous room in a block slightly away from the main hotel and it was very peaceful. There was air-conditioning thankfully and burners next to the bed to keep the mosquitoes away.

The next day, we hired a mini moke car. I had a guide-book which described all the sights on the island and during the course of the first five days, we saw all of them. The weather was extremely changeable given the time of year. It would be bright one moment and then there would be a wild electric storm and then the air would be fresh again. The east coast of the island was very windy, but there was no development there. It was completely unspoilt, and really beautiful.

At the end of the first week, I suddenly developed a raging temperature and a very sore throat. The next day, I was even worse. Tim called a doctor and he said that I had bronchitis. I felt so terrible that we decided to change our flight and go home the next day.

Before we got married, we had spent several months looking for a flat to buy. An agent rang me at work one day and said that he had an interesting flat in South Kensington which was reasonably priced. We were not impressed. It was on the fourth floor with no lift and the decoration was tatty and cheap. I peered out of the window towards a mansion block on the other side of the road, saying to Tim that the flats over there looked lovely. As we were leaving, we passed an estate agent which had photographs of many local flats in the window. There was one in the block that we had spotted. The price was slightly higher than we wanted to pay, but we agreed that I would look at it anyway.

It was the flat of my dreams. The people who owned it had recently refurbished it and had done a brilliant job. We could move into it without having to do anything, which would be a relief. Tim offered two thousand pounds less than the asking price, but the owner would only accept the full amount. We agreed to offer him that and he said he would like to think about it overnight. I was so anxious, I could hardly sleep. I had set my heart on getting that flat. It had to be that one. The next day, he came back to us and said that another person had offered the asking price too, but if we increased our offer by two thousand pounds, we could have it. Although we were absolutely at our financial limit, we managed to find the extra money. Our solicitor was able to exchange contracts in a week. I pushed him hard as I was worried that the owner would gazump us. I knew we would be poor for a while, but I did not care. Tim and I were starting a new life together.

The day we returned from our honeymoon, we splurged on a taxi from the airport as I was in no fit state to go on the train. When we got to our front door, Tim suddenly lifted me up in his arms and carried me across the threshold of our new home. I was feeling terrible as I had not been able to sleep on the plane, but I was so thrilled to be home in our new flat that I forgot how bad I felt.

The burden of the mortgage was so heavy that we had virtually no money left to live on. I used to spend hours searching through cookery books for tasty but cheap dishes to make. Meat was far too expensive even to contemplate and so we ate red peppers stuffed with rice and nuts, vegetarian lasagne, salads and mushroom risotto with a few prawns thrown in every now and then as a treat. We were very healthy as a result. My parents had recently become vegetarian and so I would exchange ideas with my mother.

Tim was still embroiled in his accountancy studies and would be for another year, so he used to sit in the kitchen and do his work each evening after supper whilst I either read a book in the sitting room or watched television. The windows in the sitting room and our bedroom were very large, but we could not afford curtains. I could have made them myself, but the major part of the expenditure was the fabric itself. We decided that we would just have to put up with it. We always woke up early as our bedroom faced east and, as it was the summer, the sun came streaming in through the window at 5 a.m. each morning.

At weekends, Tim had to work for his exams and so I used to go out with an old school friend of mine. We saw every art exhibition in town over the course of those few months and we often went to theatre matinées and sat in the cheapest seats. Sometimes we would go shopping, but we could not afford to buy anything so we just window shopped. Tim would generally take Sunday afternoons off and we would often go for walks in Hyde Park or go to Chiswick House or Syon Park. The only other break he allowed himself was on Monday evenings when we used to go to the cinema. Tickets were half price on a Monday. Life was very easy then. We had no real responsibilities. There was work and relaxation and the odd bit of cleaning and ironing to think about.

Shortly after I got married, Leonard Licht called me into a meeting room. I was surprised as I had had very little to do with him whilst I had been on the marketing team. Leonard said that he had spoken to Stephen Zimmerman and told him that he needed a graduate to help him. They had both decided that I would be the best person and he asked me if I would like to work with him and Tom Charlton. I was completely speechless.

'There is nothing that I would like more,' I finally said. I had thought very little about what my next career move would be because of the wedding. Out of the blue, I had been presented with the job I had longed for.

Moving to Leonard's team was the biggest break of my career and it came when I had only six months' experience. Leonard Licht was the most outstanding fund manager of his generation and I knew that I was the most fortunate graduate trainee in the industry to be given the opportunity to work with him. He had a natural talent for picking shares that were going up. He had a reputation for being demanding and of not suffering fools gladly, but this did not put me off. I was determined to show him that he had made the right choice.

Leonard would spend hours looking at company accounts, trying to find undervalued assets. The eighties was an era when many companies were asset rich and cash poor. The retail sector was one where Leonard was particularly active. He took enormous stakes for his clients in House of Fraser, Burton Group and Debenhams, convinced that there would be takeover activity in the sector. Most of these companies owned all the freeholds of their shops in those days and so were as much property companies as retailers. As the consumer boom began to take off, retail property began to rise sharply in value and the takeovers began. Leonard was a key player in most of these bids. His first reaction each time another one was announced was to buy more shares. He was always convinced that the bidder would have to pay more in the end and he was right.

The electronics sector was booming too at this time and, at one point, it represented 10 per cent of the total capitalization of the UK market. Leonard hardly owned a share in this sector. A very clever fund manager joined our team and he was the electronics analyst. He adored analysing electronics companies and he was constantly trying to persuade Leonard to invest in them.

'I saw a very interesting software company yesterday, Leonard,' he would say.

'What's the asset value?' would be the immediate response.

'Virtually nothing, but it's a brilliant team and they are really going places.'

'What's the yield on the shares?'

'Negligible because they're investing all the money back into the business.' It was clear that Leonard was not going to change his mind about technology stocks. He was right. The sector collapsed in 1985. There was too much hope value and not enough genuine talent.

Leonard was also in charge of the venture capital team who sat near us. When the Business Expansion Scheme was created in 1984, a fund was set up to allow private clients to invest in embryonic companies. The clients knew that many of the businesses would fail and they may lose the total value of their investment, but they hoped that every now and then a runaway success would pay for all the losers. The money was in and the team was busy looking at all the investment opportunities. As they were under-resourced, Leonard suggested that I should spend some time with them whilst the money was being invested. This was very exciting. I worked closely with a Dane called Andreas and together we travelled around Britain looking at hotels, garden furniture companies, manufacturers of pumps for liquid soap and specialist glass fabricators. We were looking for companies with strong management and interesting products with the potential to grow rapidly. It gave me a wonderful insight into how small businesses operate and the fragile nature of their existence.

In some ways I would have liked to stay in the venture team, but I could see that I did not have the right experience. Most of the people working in the area were qualified accountants, solicitors or had trained at 3i, a company set up by the high-street banks to invest in unquoted companies. I returned to the mainstream and was soon given a small amount of money to run for clients. Leonard believed that I had now done my apprenticeship and the only way to find out whether I was going to make a good fund manager was to let me try.

There was a very great difference between looking at a stock purely from an analytical stance and actually making a decision to buy it for a client. Each morning, I would come into the office, turn on my screen and spend the rest of the day flicking between the various pages checking the prices of the shares that I owned. At first I found it a nerve-racking experience, but soon I began to really enjoy it. I would go to the morning meeting and listen intently to my colleagues, hoping that the hint of a new idea would emerge. I would never just take someone else's word for it, however. If the story sounded good, I would go down to the library and look through the file myself to check that there was not something that had been forgotten.

Tom Charlton, the other person in Leonard's team, was shy and difficult to get to know, but we developed a close working relationship and I learned as much from him as I did from Leonard. The two were completely different in their styles. Leonard ran portfolios with relatively few shares in them and took big stakes in companies. Tom had lots of small holdings in all sorts of esoteric stocks, most of which I had never heard of, but at the core of his portfolios were reasonable weightings in the major stocks like BP, Shell and Unilever.

Tom had a clear understanding of the concept of risk and he was very good at minimizing it. He was, in effect, making sure that the bulk of his portfolios would keep his returns reasonably near to the index and that the more interesting situations would then provide the outperformance. In the early days, I tried to emulate Leonard. It seemed logical to me that if you put all your best ideas in the fund and had a meaningful percentage in each one that you were bound to outperform. I soon realized that having large holdings is painful when a stock goes wrong. If you have 4 per cent of the fund in a stock which is a negligible part of the index and it goes down by 25 per cent, it knocks 1 per cent off your performance relative to the market. As I matured as a fund manager, my style became more like Tom's, although I will never be as good as him.

It was easier to do better than the market in those days. There were companies who were barely followed by any stockbrokers. There was a computer system called Datastream which allowed us to enter certain characteristics and then it would search for companies that had them. I could ask for a list of companies, for example, that had a high net asset value per share, a high turnover, low profit and a high dividend and it would print it out.

I found small companies more interesting than large ones and I used to visit them to learn about what they actually did. It was possible to see most of their operations in a day and I found that I learnt a great deal by going round factories and talking to production managers. If the plant was at a standstill, I would ask why and if I got the reply that they had terrible problems and had lost several days of production, I knew that the company was going to find it difficult to meet its profit forecast. If, on the other hand, the production manager told me that he had so many orders that he had to put an extra shift on, then I knew that the profit forecast was likely to be exceeded.

As our team had consistently achieved outstanding returns, we began to win new funds. At times, Leonard and Tom could not cope with the number of presentations that had to be made to prospective clients and when an engineering company asked us to visit them one November, neither of them was available. The client would not give us an alternative date and so Leonard asked me to go with the marketing director.

'I can't go. It's a £70 million fund,' I said.

'You'll do a very good job. It'll be fine.'

'Won't they think that I'm too young?'

'It's a young people's business,' was Leonard's reply.

I was terribly nervous. This was an enormous fund with a large Trustee Board and I had never done a presentation before. I had spent many hours going over what I was going to say. It could not be any different to acting in a play or interviewing Michael Parkinson, but I was scared that I would let the firm down if I did a bad job. Charles, the marketing director, did the first bit of the presentation and cracked lots of jokes which went down very well. When it was my turn to speak, I was addressing a group of smiling faces and the nervousness subsided. When I got going, I found it easy to tell them about what I did every day and at the end of the presentation, I felt that I had done my best. Two days later, the pensions manager rang to say that we had won the account. I was absolutely over the moon.

When I told Leonard, he sent a graduate over the road to the wine shop to buy two bottles of champagne.

'I don't care whether you drink normally or not,' he said, 'we've got something to celebrate and you're going to have some champagne.'

For days after we had been told that we had won the new account, people kept coming up to me and congratulating me. It was a wonderful feeling. After that I regularly presented to prospective clients and I found this one of the most exciting parts of my job. Those who were able to win accounts through presentations were held in high regard by the organization. New business was the lifeblood and was the path to growth in profits, salaries and bonuses for everyone.

As a result of my interest in small companies, I was allowed to manage the Mercury Small Companies Fund when it was launched. This was a unit trust fund sold to the general public. In addition to newspaper advertising, it was important to sell it to regional stockbrokers and independent financial advisers who had large numbers of private clients who looked to them for advice on what fund to buy. I travelled all over the country during the launch period for the fund doing presentations and having one-on-one meetings. It was completely different to dealing with pension funds and added new interest to my job. I was twenty-six, but, as Leonard had promised, no one seemed worried by the fact that I was so young.

My evenings at home with Tim were spent silently working. He was still studying for his accountancy exams and I would produce note after note for Leonard on the companies that he asked me about. I also had a sector to research and I was constantly on the look-out for small companies to put in the unit trust. Leonard was always telling me what a good job I was doing and at every pay review I received a bigger increase than I had been expecting. It was wonderful to feel appreciated and it had the effect of making me try even harder as I did not want to let Leonard down in any way. I realized the importance of praising the people who work for you and I remembered this later when I got the opportunity to run a business.

Just as Tim had been happy to wait to get married, he was in no hurry to have children. I would mention it every now and then and he would say that we were too young and that we should at least wait until he had finished his accountancy exams. He pointed to the fact that most of our friends were not even married yet, never mind having children. But I had always known that I wanted to have children and I was getting impatient. The dogs at home were my surrogate children and I used to spend hours hugging them and playing with them as an outlet for my frustrated maternal instincts. I did not know whether I would carry on working if I had a child, but I knew that financially it would be tough if I did not. We were used to living on two incomes after all.

If we were going to have a baby, we would have to move as we only had one bedroom. I began to look at the property pages in the Sunday papers and one weekend something caught my eye. There was an advertisement for a two-bedroom flat in Notting Hill with potential to create three further rooms within an existing structure. I could not imagine what this meant, but I went to see it after work one evening. I made an offer on the spot and ended up buying it without Tim even seeing it. He was horrified when he discovered that it was opposite the All Saints Road, which was a haunt of drug-dealers and a no-go area in those days.

The house had originally been in the middle of a terrace, but now stood alone. The houses to the right of it had been bombed during the war and replaced with a block of flats in the sixties. A housing trust had bought up the remainder of the terrace, with the exception of this one house, with the intention of knocking it down and building a new block of flats. But the residents of the last house refused to sell which put the plans in doubt. In the end, a compromise was reached. The residents agreed to the rest of the terrace being knocked down as long as the housing trust built a buttress at the side of the remaining house and transferred ownership to them. The buttress was split into three compartments and went right up the whole building. All that needed to be done to create new rooms for each flat was to put floors, windows and doors in the buttress. I asked why the residents had not yet bothered to do anything about it; the buttress had been built three years before. There was no particular reason; it was simply inertia.

At first Tim thought I was completely mad to take on such a property, but he soon came round to the idea. When we moved in, I arranged for a residents' meeting and persuaded the other occupants of the house that we should go ahead and convert the buttress all at once. I volunteered to do all the administrative work and spent several months planning it with the surveyor and getting tender documents prepared. Eventually, the builders arrived. It had sounded great on paper, but when they were actually traipsing through our flats and creating endless dust, it became a nightmare.

In the middle of all this, I began to feel very unwell. I felt sick and had terrible headaches. I am very healthy and seldom visit a doctor, but I was forced to do so. He looked in my eyes, ears and throat, but could find nothing wrong with me. He did a urine test and a blood test and eventually came up with a diagnosis. I was pregnant! The building project had got under way and the contractor had been chosen. The men would be arriving shortly and we would soon be living in a nasty dusty mess. I had not been actively trying to get pregnant and it was a very inconvenient moment to be told that I was. Depression soon gave way to elation. This was what I had really wanted. A baby was on the way.

five

When journalists interview me now, there seems to be a presumption that I sat down one day and mapped out my life plan. They imagine that I knew from the beginning that I wanted five children and that I had a burning ambition to get to the top of my profession as quickly as possible. That is not how it happened. Life is not so easy to plan. I knew I wanted at least two children, but I never thought I would have five and I had no idea whether I would still be working a few years down the line or not.

I did not do biology at school. Sex education was not part of the curriculum either. When I got pregnant with Georgie, I was twenty-five and had no idea what changes my body was going through or how quickly the baby was developing. The flat was a building site and it was unlikely that we would be rid of the men before the baby arrived. It was not really a suitable area for children and nannies either. I had bought the flat because I had seen the opportunity to make money. I was certain that we would and I knew that we would be able to sell it easily and move to a better area when it was finished.

My mother and father were absolutely thrilled to hear the news, as were Tim's parents. My baby was to be the first grandchild for my parents and the third for Tim's. At forty-seven, my mother would be a very young granny. She had always wished that she had had more than two children, but she belonged to a generation that worried about the population explosion and believed that it was socially irresponsible to do anything other than replace themselves. The prospect of a grandchild was, therefore, very welcome.

The minute that I am pregnant, I want to tell everyone, but I was dreading breaking the news to Leonard. I was unsure what his reaction would be. We had got into an excellent routine and he relied on me to organize the day-to-day running of the team.

We sat in a completely open-plan office and I did not feel that it was the sort of issue I could discuss with him over the desk. After a couple of days of plucking up courage, I asked if I could have a word with him in a quiet room. He was delighted when I told him. I said that I intended to return to work and, as his own wife also had children and a career, he did not doubt me.

When I thought about what I wanted to do with my life during my university years, I was not conscious of confronting the issue of how I would fit a career in with marriage and children. It all seemed so remote. But now I had to face the issue. I was pregnant. It did not seem viable to stop working and then try and get back in several years down the line. I was not well enough established in my profession to be able to do that. Tim's final exams were only a few weeks away and, once he was qualified, his earning power would increase significantly. I was sure that he would pass first time even though the pass rate was less than 50 per cent. But did I want to spend the rest of my life financially dependent on him?

My mother has never thought of herself as being a role model for me because she has never been in paid employment. She did not go to university, despite her excellent A level grades, because she got married so young. But when I was seven and my brother was five, she applied to the Liverpool School of Architecture and was accepted in the face of fierce competition. She was only twenty-eight, but she counted as a mature student.

After a day of lectures, she would return home and cook for us, bath us, listen to us reading and then read to us. Then she would return to her studying. Some nights she would stay up until three or four in the morning making models of buildings and then ironing my school uniform before going to bed. She looked permanently exhausted and yet she managed to do everything well. She was beautifully dressed, she was a brilliant cook, she was a good mother and a diligent student. As a child, what I saw was a woman who was juggling many different roles and doing all of them well. There was little time to enjoy herself, but she was fulfilled.

Although my mother had decided not to go on to practise architecture when she was qualified, she encouraged me to keep working. She had wanted to be there for my brother and me, but it was not long before we were both at boarding school. She was still under forty when I went to university. One of the reasons that she had not pursued a career was because my father took a rather old-fashioned view of women and work. He felt that it was his duty to provide for his wife and children and that a mother's place was in the home. My mother had told me that he had not wanted her to work and I had found this difficult to understand. He had always told me that he wanted me to have the same opportunities as my brother and he had made sure that I had had the best possible education. What would be the point of not using it? When I announced that I was pregnant, the whole debate was opened up and I could see that my mother was right. My father made it quite plain that he thought I should stay at home.

When I discussed the issue with Tim, he was in no doubt: I would be impossible to live with if I gave up work. He knew that the monotony of staying at home would be difficult for me to cope with. He would not have liked to do it and he did not see why I should either.

'What will you do when they have all grown up and left home if you give up work?' he asked. 'Go to coffee mornings? Go shopping? I think you would get pretty bored.' It was important to gather everyone's views, but I was determined to keep an open mind on the subject until I had experienced motherhood. I wanted to try to do both and I had told Leonard that I was going back, but I knew that when I had spent some time with the baby, I would be in a better position to judge what was possible.

When I discovered that I was pregnant, I had to choose whether to have the baby privately or on the NHS. Since none of my friends had children yet, I felt like a pioneer. My GP explained what would happen if I chose the NHS:

long waits in clinics, no guarantee of seeing the same midwife each time and only seeing the consultant if something went wrong. If I went privately, I would always see the consultant and I could have the appointments in the early evening which meant that I would not have to take time off work. Because I am an avid supporter of the NHS, it was difficult for me to decide on the private route, but I realized that the flexibility was vital if my job was to be unaffected. I was as committed to my work as I had always been and I did not want my pregnancy to interfere with it unnecessarily. I could see no reason why I could not work right up to the point when the baby was due and I still went to visit companies until the end of my eighth month. The personnel department were a little concerned about this, but I convinced them that since I had builders in the flat, I was better off at work. It was agreed that I would stop one week before the due date unless, of course, the baby came early.

For the last week before the baby was born, we stayed with Tim's cousin and his wife who lived near us in Notting Hill as our flat was uninhabitable. On Saturday 18 October 1986, I wandered back to the flat with Tim to start putting books on to our new bookshelves. We were having an Indian summer and it was extremely hot. I was feeling very weighed down and uncomfortable. The baby was due two days later and I had dutifully packed my overnight bag which was sitting in Tim's cousin's flat. We spent a happy couple of hours moving books between the bedroom and the sitting room. At 5 p.m., I bent down to pick up some more books and my waters broke.

'Help! Help!' I shrieked at Tim.

We rang the hospital in a state of high excitement and they told us to come in straight away. They would inform the consultant.

We rushed over to Tim's cousin's flat to collect my bag. He and two friends were watching some sporting event on the television and his wife was out.

'We're off to the hospital. The baby's on the way,' I said.

'Good luck!' they shouted after us as we left the flat. I still had not had a contraction and I felt absolutely fine.

We arrived at the Portland Hospital at 6 p.m. and were shown to the birthing suite. The midwife asked if we would like something to eat. I was feeling a little peckish so we ordered some sandwiches. We watched the television and chatted merrily, not realizing what horrors were about to come.

At 7 p.m., I was violently sick and then suddenly found myself doubled up in pain (as far as one can be at nine months pregnant). It was the most terrible pain that I had ever experienced. It was all consuming. Tim looked really worried and called the midwife who attached monitors to me and explained to Tim how the gas and air worked. Again I was thrown into turmoil as another contraction began and Tim placed the mask of the gas and air cylinder over my face and told me to breathe in. The combination of the shock and the gas made me temporarily lose consciousness. A few minutes later, I came round to find a woman doctor examining me. I was only three centimetres dilated. Another seven centimetres to go before I could try to push the baby out. How would I survive?

I remembered vividly the lady who took our ante-natal classes telling us that labour pains were akin to bad period pains. Many people had told me this and I now knew that it was garbage. I am sure that the reason epidurals are so commonplace is because most women have been misled in this way and are thrown into a state of shock when they have the first few contractions. It feels as if your body is being torn in half and you cannot imagine how you are going to survive. But our teacher was right about one thing: I found that when I managed to relax and do my breathing exercises, I slipped into a kind of trance.

I was determined to give birth without an epidural, but not because I was brave. In fact, it was the reverse. As a law student, I had read a number of medical negligence cases in which epidurals had gone wrong and left women paralysed from the waist down. The procedure has greatly improved over the years and there is a minimal risk in having one now, but why do it if your body can cope by itself? If the pain really was too much to bear, no one would ever have more than one child. I have been lucky enough to give birth to five children without any complications and so an epidural has never been necessary.

At the end of the first hour I was beginning to relax and cope with the terrible pain. By the end of the second hour, I was slipping into a trance. Earlier, I had done quite a lot of screaming and the midwife had told me to be quiet as I was going to wake up the whole hospital. I found this rather strange as I thought women were supposed to scream in labour. Anyway, I could not help it.

Eventually, the consultant arrived. He examined me, said

that it would still be some time before I was ready to push the baby out and disappeared. The midwife came in and said that my brother was outside the door and did I want to see him.

'No!' I said emphatically. How could she think that I wanted to see anyone in my current state? Tim went to see him and found his twin brother, William, lying asleep on the sofa outside the door with a bottle of champagne in his hand. It was 11.30 p.m. and William had been doing some advance celebrating. He stirred as Tim approached and said that he wanted to be the first person to see his twin brother's baby.

By midnight, the cervix was ten centimetres dilated and I was ready to push. The consultant returned. The midwife held one leg and Tim held the other. After forty-five minutes of little progress, the consultant began to get impatient.

'You're wasting those contractions. Push, girl, push!' Fifteen minutes later, he threatened me with forceps if I did not try harder. I was exhausted and angry that he was being so unsympathetic. The pushing just did not seem to come naturally to me. At the ante-natal classes, we had been told that when the cervix was fully dilated, we would get this overwhelming urge to push. Five babies later, I can say that I have never felt that urge.

I finally got the hang of the pushing and at 1.30 a.m. on Sunday 19 October 1986, my daughter, my first born, was placed on my tummy. She had a small amount of strawberry-blonde hair and a round, chubby face. She was adorable. I clasped her in my arms and kissed her. Tim wiped a tear from his eye as he peered at his new baby.

'Who do you look like?' he said. She did not look anything like her parents. She was a cross between my father and Tim's twin brother. Georgina Suzanna Louise weighed 8 lb 13 oz. All the nurses kept commenting on how large she was, especially for a first baby, but she seemed minute to me.

Georgie was taken away to be cleaned up and I was put in a wheelchair and taken to a proper room. William woke up as the door opened and leapt to his feet.

'What is it?'

'A girl,' we replied in unison. 'Her name's Georgina and she looks like you.'

We were sipping champagne when Georgie was returned to us and Tim showed her off proudly to his twin brother. He lifted her up and sat in a chair cuddling her. I smiled. Tim had not shown much real interest in babies before and I had not really known what reception our baby would get. As Tim was one of four boys, I had been convinced that Georgie was a boy and we had called her Henry throughout the pregnancy. Tim had once told me that he had always wanted a sister and he was clearly delighted that he had a little girl.

After half an hour of celebration, William and Tim departed. Georgie had fallen asleep in Tim's arms and had been returned to her perspex cot. I felt so elated that I could not even contemplate sleep. The horrific pain had all been worthwhile. I felt very sore still, but I had a beautiful baby to show for it. I put on the headphones of my Walkman and listened to Mozart's *Don Giovanni*. It was suitably uplifting. Eventually, I fell asleep, but only a couple of hours later a lady appeared in the room with the breakfast tray.

The day began with my first attempt at breast feeding. Some women take to it like ducks to water and do not seem to suffer from sore nipples. Those with fair skin tend to have more trouble. Nipples were obviously tougher in ancient times when they were exposed more to the elements and clothing fabrics were rougher. Even after having my fifth child, I still had to endure days of agony at the beginning. It is worth persevering though. Once breast feeding is going well, there is nothing more satisfying than sitting with a baby attached to you. When they are very little, they stare straight ahead as though they are about to be deprived of all nourishment for ever. As they get older, they look into their mummy's eyes with a look of utter devotion and there is nothing more wonderful.

When you have your first baby, your life changes for ever. You cannot do anything on impulse. Before I arranged anything, I had to think how it would fit in with Georgie's routine. The first time that I went shopping, I realized that I could not push the pram and the trolley at the same time. I went to John Lewis in search of a solution and bought a baby carrier. Small babies love being transported in this manner, it is reminiscent of the cosiness of the womb and they can hear their mother's heartbeat. Georgie would go to sleep whilst I did the shopping, walked in the park or went to the library.

When I had decided that I wanted to return to work after the baby was born, I had to think about the issue of child-care. I soon realized that the cost of it was phenomenal. I began by examining all the options. Warburgs did not have a crèche, but there was an American bank in the City that had set up one recently and there were a number of places for children of non-employees. I thought about this option, but quickly dismissed it. I could not contemplate taking my baby on the tube with me in the morning crush and then leaving her in an air-conditioned office block with no fresh air and no playground.

I did not like the idea of a nursery either, but I felt that I should find out what they could offer. One positive point was that my baby would be with other children which would allow her to develop social skills, learn to share toys and possibly gain more stimulation than with a nanny or a childminder. Some mothers worry that if they leave their child with a nanny or childminder, they will reject their mother and that her position in the child's affections will be usurped. This did not concern me, but it was true that in a nursery my baby would have a variety of carers and this sort of individual attachment would be unlikely to develop. Nannies and childminders have to do household chores whereas helpers at nurseries can spend virtually all their time playing with the children and so it was possible that my baby would get more attention. I knew that nurseries have to be registered with the Social Services department of the relevant local authority and they are subject to regular inspection; this was a source of comfort.

For me, the disadvantages outweighed the advantages.

The good nurseries were heavily oversubscribed and the cost was high. Most were only open from 8 a.m. to 6 p.m. and I had to leave for work at 7.15 a.m. and would not get home until 6.30 p.m., so there was not the flexibility on hours that one gets with a childminder or a nanny. I was keen that my baby should get into a good routine which I thought would be difficult in a nursery environment where each carer looked after three babies and mine would just have to fit in.

I discovered that childminders tended to be considerably cheaper than nannies. The fact that most childminders have children of their own would mean that my baby would have someone to play with. I have a friend who has used the same childminder for many years. Her husband had been married before and had an older son, but he did not live with them. Their daughter was, therefore, in effect an only child. The childminder was a mother herself with two daughters, and over the years they became like sisters to my friend's daughter. Even when her daughter was old enough to go home from school by herself, she would still go to her childminder regularly. I could see the attractions of a childminder, but the problem was that there were not many in central London.

I came to the conclusion that the best option for me would be to employ a nanny. It would give me the greatest flexibility and mean that I did not have to worry about dropping the baby off in the morning or collecting in the evening. I could see that there would be a problem with all the other options if the baby was ever sick. It might only be a heavy cold and a slight temperature, but in those circumstances it would be difficult to put the baby in the car and drop her off with a childminder or at a nursery.

Having decided that I was going to employ a nanny, I rang up all the agencies and was horrified by the level of their fees. So I put an advert in the *Lady*. There were two replies that merited further investigation and I invited both of them to be interviewed. The first was extremely quiet and rather prim. She did not smile once during the hour that Tim and I spent talking to her. The second was exactly the opposite. She was from Liverpool, very friendly and seemed great fun.

Interviewing a nanny is very difficult, especially if your first baby has not even arrived yet. I did not know how I would look after the baby, never mind how I would want someone else to. I did feel, though, that it would be important for the baby to go for walks and make friends with other babies in the area. I also wanted someone who was going to keep the house tidy and look after the baby clothes properly. I cannot stand dirty kitchens and I knew that I would not be able to live with someone who did not keep mine clean.

Many of the questions that you ask give away the answers that you expect. For example, if you say, 'Would you take the baby to the park every day?' the reply is likely to be, 'Oh yes. I am a great walker. I will take the baby out every day.' That's good, you think. This is just the person for me.

The girl from Liverpool gave all the right answers. I was convinced that we had got a gem. When Georgie arrived, I rang her and she came to see her new charge in the hospital.

She cuddled her and cooed at her. I noticed then that she smelt of smoke despite the fact that she had told us in the interview that she was a non-smoker, but I thought that she must have been sitting next to someone who was smoking on the bus. I had arranged to go and stay with my mother for a week when we left the hospital and so we agreed that she would get everything ready for our return. There were a number of outfits that needed washing and ironing and she could spend some time moving her things in and sorting out her room.

After Georgie and I had been discharged from the hospital, Tim drove us to Cheshire to my parents' house. He stayed for the first couple of nights and then had to return to work. He had passed his accountancy exams and was now involved in the audit of a major public company and could not take time off. On the second day after the nanny had started, he was on his way from the office to his client and had to stop at the flat to collect something that he had forgotten. The nanny had no prior warning. He opened the door and found her in the sitting room with a friend smoking. There was a child on the floor. When he went into our bedroom, he found another child asleep in our bed. Furious, he fired her and told her to leave immediately. He rang me to tell me what had happened and I felt betrayed.

After this disaster, I decided that I would look after Georgie by myself for the first few weeks and then recruit a nanny just before I was due to return to work. It did not need two people to look after one small baby and it would save a lot of money if I waited. I was tempted to stay with my mother for more than a week, but our flat was now ready and I was missing Tim. He drove back up to fetch Georgie and me.

The first day that he left me in the flat with Georgie and went to work dragged terribly. I was absolutely besotted with her, but very small babies are only interested in eating and sleeping and so I soon became bored and lonely. All my friends were at work and I did not know anyone else who had a baby. In retrospect, I would have been better off going to the National Childbirth Trust ante-natal classes instead of those provided by the hospital. My sister-in-law did this when she was expecting her first child and made some firm friendships with other first-time mothers who lived near her.

For company, I used to drive Tim to work and collect him every day from his clients' offices which were down the M40 and inaccessible by public transport. Despite the fact that I was about to go on maternity leave, I had been promoted and given my first company car and I loved driving it. Georgie would sleep all the way there and back, although one day she seemed to have some sort of tummyache and screamed both ways.

Georgie was born in mid-October and by mid-November I was positively looking forward to returning to work in January. I had all my post sent home every other day and, after I had read the *Financial Times* from cover to cover, I would sort through the stockbrokers' notes and read about as many companies as I could. I really missed the buzz of the office and felt very remote from what was going on, but by reading as much as I could at least I was maintaining my overall knowledge base.

I needed to find another nanny and this time I was determined to employ someone who was likely to stay with us for a long time. After the error I had made with the first one, I doubted my ability to choose the right person and so I got my parents to help me. I rang up all the agencies and again put an advert in the *Lady*. I had three or four possibles, but two were not suitable as they were just out of college. I arranged to interview the others.

Experience had made me more circumspect and I was rigorous in my questioning. My father was very helpful in suggesting how I should structure the interviews. The first girl arrived and I asked her what she would plan each day and she said all the right things. She would find a playgroup to take Georgie to and meet some other children of the same age. She would cook a good lunch for her every day with lots of vegetables and she would take her for walks. She was well turned out and very polite, but she was rather dull. We all agreed that, although she seemed to be a responsible girl and I would have no worries about leaving Georgie in her care, she lacked personality.

In total contrast to the first, the second girl had a big personality. Her name was Lynne and she came from Wolverhampton. She bounced into the house and greeted us all with a warm smile. She alighted on Georgie, asked if she could hold her and then spent some time talking to her and cuddling her. She gave similar answers to the first girl, but spoke about what she would be doing with much greater enthusiasm. She said that she had a great nanny friend who was working a couple of streets away with a family whose baby was about the same age as Georgie. After Lynne had left, my father said she reminded him of his nanny, Elsie, who had looked after him for the first eight years of his life. I asked her to come back and meet Tim and then offered her the job.

Some of those in authority at Warburgs had been sceptical about whether I would return. Leonard was pretty confident that I would, but as our client base was growing strongly, he had been encouraged by others to recruit another experienced person to work with Tom and me. I was rather cross about this, especially as the person who was hired was brought in at a higher level than me, but this just made me all the more determined to prove that I could combine a baby and work.

Before I went on maternity leave I had been given two new sectors to research: brewers and distillers and food manufacturing. Lynne arrived in December, giving me more time to spend getting to know the companies that I was going to follow. My secretary sent me packs of information and I waded through them, trying to learn as much as I could before I returned to work.

One morning, the telephone rang. It was Carol Galley. Carol had been very supportive throughout my pregnancy and was not in the camp that thought I would not be coming back. She said that she had arranged a meeting with Ernest Saunders and Olivier Roux at Guinness to discuss how the integration of Distillers, a large whisky company which Guinness had recently bought, was going. As the new analyst on the sector, she wanted me to write the briefing note and come to the meeting. I was very pleased that she had asked me even though I was still on maternity leave.

Life suddenly had a clear purpose. The monotony of looking after Georgie and counting the hours until Tim was due to return home was broken. I already had much of what I needed to write the briefing note and so, after going through it all, I began to identify the major issues that we needed to discuss at the meeting. Within a week, my note was finished. I typed it myself on my electric typewriter and then sent it to my secretary to circulate. This was to be my first business meeting since I had had Georgie. I was in a terrible panic about what to wear as none of my old work clothes fitted. I could not go in a maternity dress and so I had to go and buy something.

The day before we were due to see Guinness, I turned on the radio to listen to the news as I was preparing Georgie's lunch. The first item was that the DTI had swooped on Guinness's offices early that morning and seized a number of documents relating to the company's bid for Distillers. I rang the office and spoke to Carol's secretary. She said that Carol thought that the meeting would be cancelled, but she would get back to me when she had a definitive answer. An hour later, she rang to say that the meeting was still on.

I went to the office first for the pre-meet and then we got a taxi to Guinness's offices near Marble Arch. We all felt rather apprehensive. When we arrived, we were shown into the boardroom. There was a vast table surrounded by black leather chairs. One chair was a great deal larger than the others and we joked that we had better not sit in it as it must be Ernest's chair. We waited for about ten minutes and then the door flew open and Ernest Saunders walked in, greeting Carol Galley warmly.

'Sit down!' he said and walked round the table to the enormous chair. Olivier Roux and another of the Guinness directors were with him. We managed to go through the whole meeting, which took seventy-five minutes, without mentioning the DTI raid the previous day. It was clearly an important issue for us as shareholders, but it was difficult to know how to bring it up. Ernest seemed quite relaxed and completely in control. He was behaving as if nothing had happened.

When we had covered all the points that we had planned to raise, the meeting concluded and we were invited to have a drink in another room. All the whisky brands were prominently displayed together with cans of Guinness. We all opted for soft drinks. It was only at that point that the DTI investigation became a topic of conversation. Ernest had clearly been taken totally by surprise, but he said that he was confident that no irregularities would be found.

My first full day back at work was 2 January, ten weeks after Georgie had been born. In the back of my mind, I knew that if Georgie was not happy, I would have to give up. I had every faith in Lynne, but I could not stop myself ringing her several times during the day.

'How long did she sleep for? Did she take all her milk from the bottle? Are you going for a walk this afternoon?'

I would look at my watch and wonder why the day was going so slowly. When it was time to go, I would rush home and pick up my darling Georgie and hug her. She was still so tiny. How could I leave her every day? I had many moments of doubt and I would frequently say to Tim that I thought I should stop working. When Georgie was about five months old, she went through a phase of refusing to come to me when I got home and putting her arms out to Lynne. I was so upset that she did not want me that I spent the evening crying and saying that I had to give up. Tim told me not to be ridiculous. He said that it would all settle down soon.

Tim was right. We got into a regular routine. I would get Georgie up in the morning and give her milk and then hand her over to Lynne. When I came back at about 6.15 p.m., I would bath her and then feed her. I was a typical first-time mother. Every time I put Georgie in her cot, she would scream and so I used to lie on the bed with her and cuddle her until she went to sleep. I was so tired that invariably I would fall asleep too and Tim would have to wake me gently and transfer Georgie to her cot when he came home. This went on until she was about fifteen months old.

Having a child brings with it a large amount of extra administration. I had to think about schools for Georgie as soon as she was born. I had to take her to the doctor to be vaccinated and for her developmental checks. Lynne had to be paid. I had to make sure that there was food in the fridge at all times for both of them. There was a panic when we were going on holiday and I realized that I had not put her on my passport. Georgie kept growing and so I had to find time to buy her new clothes. There were twice as many things to pack when we went away. As she got older, I had to ferry her backwards and forwards to parties and when she went to school there were school plays, concerts and sports day to attend. And now there is an endless amount of homework . . .

Tim had little to do with most of this extra work and so it fell fairly and squarely on me. There were some things that I could delegate to Lynne, but the vast majority of them had to be done by me. Trying to combine a full-time job with being a mother was very exhausting and I soon realized that it required good organization. I never used to write lists of things to do before Georgie arrived, but I found that this was the only way to make sure that I did not forget anything. I also had to develop the ability to think about work when I was there and Georgie when I was at home. I could not have played either role properly if I had allowed the two to merge into each other.

Once I had got used to being a mother and a fund manager, the fact that I was doing both was barely percep-tible to my colleagues. Lynne was doing a great job and I had no worries about Georgie. Most days I would ring to find out how she was, but if I did not have time, it did not matter. Leonard gave me more responsibility and I was effectively running the team on a day-to-day basis. I organized everything. We had added some international fund managers and there were now ten of us in total. We were gaining new clients and the performance of our funds was excellent. I could leave at 5.45 p.m. each night without any feelings of guilt. I had worked intensively through the day and had usually completed everything on my list.

Occasionally I would have to take something home and work on it after Georgie had gone to sleep.

I knew that I could only do my job properly if I had a reliable nanny and Lynne was excellent. When Georgie was nine months old, we moved from Notting Hill to Little Venice. Lynne was unhappy about the move as she had made so many friends and she did not want to leave them behind. It was not that far away, but she could not drive and the public transport between the new flat and the old was not good. None the less, she said that she was happy to stay because she loved Georgie so much. She soon made new friends, but I became concerned when she started going out until the early hours of the morning during the week. She took no notice when I suggested that she should confine these activities to the weekends. After a number of heated discussions, we parted company and I replaced her with a pretty Welsh girl called Sara.

I had coped with one child and had continued to make progress with my career. Georgie loved Sara and she was a sensible girl whom I could rely on totally. She had a boyfriend who was in the army in Germany and so there were no late-night escapades as there had been with Lynne. When Georgie was fifteen months old, Tim and I thought that it was time to think about having a second child. Again, I worked right through the pregnancy. I stopped work on the day that Alice was due and was annoyed when she was nine days late. I was wasting my precious maternity leave. Georgie and Sara continued with their normal routine and so I was left at home by myself much of the time.

I assured Leonard that I would be returning to work when the baby was born. I think he believed me because he promoted me to the rank of assistant director just before I was due to have the baby. But, as before, I was determined to keep an open mind. I wanted to go on working, but if I felt that the children were suffering in any way, I would give up.

My senior colleagues were again sceptical about whether I would return and persuaded Leonard to embark upon another recruiting exercise. The team had grown significantly as a result of internal additions, but they felt that another senior person was needed. Leonard did the interviewing and then invited me to have lunch with the person he had chosen. He was a very pleasant chap and I did not object to him being employed, but it did rather irritate me that the response to me having a baby always seemed to be to hire someone. Obviously it made sense from a business point of view, but it was a bit like digging a grave before someone has died.

We ended up having a baby and moving house at the same time. As if that was not bad enough, Tim had just changed jobs too. He was in the middle of his first deal at his new firm, Kleinwort Benson, when Alice arrived. It was a drab November day and I had my first contraction at midday. I immediately rang Tim and told him to come and take me to the hospital. When we arrived, he picked up the telephone and started talking to a lawyer about the deal. After half an hour, he put the telephone down, oblivious to the fact that I was in agony, and announced that he was hungry and he was going to get a sandwich.

'You can't go. The baby might be born whilst you're out,' I said through gritted teeth.

'It won't be here for hours,' he said and wandered off to Marks and Spencer on the Edgware Road. Alice was born minutes after he returned.

Alice was the perfect baby. She slept through the night when she was only a few weeks old and hardly ever cried. Leonard was throwing a party for his wife's fortieth birthday two weeks after she had arrived. We had moved into our new house in Wandsworth that week and everything was in chaos. I knew that Leonard really wanted me to go to the party and I was determined not to let him down. I thought about taking Alice with me and leaving her in a bedroom, but because she was so good and slept every evening, I decided to leave her at home. Tim and I drove to Highgate expecting to be able to stay for at least a couple of hours, but shortly after we had arrived, Sara rang to say that Alice was awake and beginning to whinge. I was kicking myself. I knew that I should have brought her with us. Sara thought it was possible that she would go back to sleep and said she would ring us if she did not. Just as we sat down to dinner, I was called to the telephone again. I could hear hysterical screams in the background. Tim and I jumped in the car and drove back to Wandsworth at high speed.

Georgie loved Alice and showed no signs of jealousy. I went back to work and found that there was little difference between having one and two children. The big change had come when Georgie had arrived. All would have been fine, but Sara had decided to get married and was going to go and live in Germany. I was in a state of high anxiety. I could only do my job properly if I had a good, experienced nanny and I knew from my own and other people's experience that they were not easy to come by.

I contacted all the agencies well in advance of Sara's departure, but it became apparent that most nannies wanted jobs that started immediately. I came across a nanny called Joan who was older and had been looking after children since she was seventeen. I met her in February and thought that she was the best nanny that I had ever come across. I was desperate for her to come and look after Georgie and Alice and I asked if she would mind temping until May. She said that she really liked us, but she wanted to get settled as soon as she could and so she took another job.

Luck was on my side. Just before Sara was due to get married, Joan rang me and asked if the job was still available as the one she had taken had not worked out. She came to live with us in May 1989 and is still with us after eight years. It is impossible to do a responsible job unless you have an absolutely reliable nanny. Joan is a latter-day Mary Poppins who anticipates my every thought and has outstanding organizational skills. The first day that I left the children with her and went to work, I returned to a spotless, tidy house, the children were bathed and she was reading to them. I opened a drawer in Georgie's room and everything had been reorganized. The children's clothes were meticulously ironed and looked like new.

Our house in Wandsworth had five bedrooms and a large garden. After living in flats for years, it felt enormous. We had a Mercedes estate to carry our two children round

London with all their gear and both Tim and I had excellent jobs. I was twenty-eight and had recently been made a divisional director. Tim was a corporate financier working for a leading merchant bank. We had two lovely children. I thought we had it all.

six

Every mother is relieved when her baby is delivered with ten fingers and ten toes and everything else looks normal. The worries of pregnancy vanish and you think that the child will have the gift of good health as of right. As a small child, Georgie was exceptionally healthy and never had anything wrong with her apart from the occasional cold.

In April 1989, when Georgie was two and a half and Alice was five months old, we went on holiday to Portugal. Georgie had always loved going on holiday and, in particular, flying. When we took off from Heathrow for Faro, she suddenly burst into tears and started screaming. I was surprised and tried all forms of bribery, but she would not settle down. Other passengers looked at me with disapproval, but there was nothing that I could do to stop Georgie's agonizing screams. Once we arrived in Portugal, she seemed to improve and I thought that she must have had some sort of earache. Friends had told me that they had had problems with their children's ears when they were flying and this was the most plausible explanation.

We reached our villa and all seemed to be well, but the

next day, Georgie's temperature shot up. I called a local doctor who spoke impeccable English and examined her thoroughly. He said that she had bronchitis and prescribed an antibiotic. Georgie was unwell for the rest of our week in Portugal, but because her temperature stayed down, I was not too concerned. I could not have known that this illness would mark the beginning of the decline in Georgie's overall health and the start of my quest to find out what was wrong with her. It had never occurred to me that I would ever be faced with having to look after a seriously ill child.

A mother generally knows when her child is unwell. You know their little ways and very few children are hypochondriacs. Some diseases, however, are difficult to diagnose and many GPs never see a case of, for example, leukaemia in a child during their whole careers. Obtaining a diagnosis when you know that there is something wrong with your child can be a problem.

Georgie had a number of illnesses over the following months and seemed to be getting paler. Periodically, she complained that her legs hurt and sometimes she would crawl around the floor saying that she could not walk. I went with her to see several GPs in our NHS practice and I also took her to a private GP in the West End. All said that she had a virus. Occasionally they identified a bacterial infection and prescribed an antibiotic. It was clear to me that they all thought I was a neurotic mother. Joan had more than twenty years' experience of caring for children and I asked her what she thought was wrong with Georgie.

She said that increasingly she was beginning to think that she was just being naughty. Perhaps I was being neurotic.

In early August, Tim and I had to go to a wedding and left Georgie and Alice with Joan for the day. She took them to Battersea Park where Georgie jumped off a small roundabout and fell to the ground clasping her leg. Joan ran to help her up, but Georgie could not stand. Joan thought that she must have twisted her ankle and found a Parks Policeman to give them a lift to the car park. When they got in the car, Georgie still seemed to be in great pain so Joan, who was very worried by this time, took her to the casualty department at St George's Hospital in Tooting. After a long wait, a junior doctor said it was just a sprain and sent her away.

Over the next few weeks, Georgie seemed to improve. At the end of August, I had to go to New York on business for a few days. This was unusual as my work was predominantly UK based. When I returned, I was struck by how pale Georgie looked. Joan said that she had been a little under the weather, but not serious enough to warrant a visit to the doctor. I wanted a doctor to see her just to make sure as we were going on holiday to Scotland the following week.

Again we were told by our local GP that Georgie was fine. A few days later, she had a raging temperature and lay in her bed looking as white as the sheets. I was very worried and rang the private GP that we had seen before. I asked the receptionist if the doctor would be prepared to make a home visit, but I was told that he only did this in exceptional circumstances. I insisted that this was an exceptional circumstance and she put me through so that I could explain the situation to the doctor directly. He agreed reluctantly to come and see Georgie. His parting sentence was: 'This is going to cost you a lot of money.' I was not concerned about the cost. All I wanted was to know what was wrong with my daughter.

When the doctor arrived and examined Georgie, he informed me that there was nothing particularly wrong with her. Possibly she had a virus, but it was nothing to worry about. When I asked why she was so pale, he said that children often looked pale.

'She eats a proper diet doesn't she?' I nodded. 'Well then,' he said and left making no effort to hide his irritation at having been called out.

A couple of days passed and Georgie seemed to get a little better, although she still looked very pale. She had a number of bruises on her body in funny places and her gums bled when we brushed her teeth. Nevertheless, we thought she was well enough to go to Scotland and so I set off for Heathrow with Georgie, Alice and the luggage and met Tim, who had come straight from work. Georgie's behaviour on the aeroplane to Inverness was just as it had been when we went to Portugal. Again, the other passengers looked at me with fierce disapproval. One of the flight attendants came up to me at one point and asked if there was anything that she could do to help. She said to me: 'She looks ever so pale. Is there something wrong with her?'

The week that we spent in Scotland was horrific. Georgie

cried endlessly, refused to walk anywhere and finally stopped eating. I have always rationed sweets in the interest of good teeth, but I bought Georgie a large bar of chocolate which she usually loved. She would not even eat that. Whenever we went in the car, she fell deeply asleep. I felt intensely frustrated that nobody would believe me, but in a way I did not want to be told what was wrong. Tim and I were both beginning to think that it was something serious.

We returned to London and I tried to ignore the fact that Georgie was not getting any better. On the afternoon of the day after our return, she was due to go back to nursery school as it was the start of the new term. That morning, I went to the West End with Georgie as I had been meaning to get a prospectus for a school there for some time. I went in, but there was no one in the school office. I had to carry Georgie as she was so weak and, as I wandered up the stairs in search of someone to ask, I bumped into the school nurse. I explained what I wanted and she said she would arrange for a prospectus to be sent to me.

'What's wrong with this little one? She's looking very pale.' I could not stop myself. The whole story of Georgie's health problems poured out and she advised me to go and demand a blood test at my doctor's surgery immediately. I knew she was right. Why had I come to the West End in the first place? I had told myself that I had to get the prospectus, but I could have rung up and asked for one to be sent. I was trying to pluck up courage to go into the doctor's surgery and ask for help. As I walked out of the school, my arms were aching from carrying Georgie. I walked very slowly in the direction of the surgery. I kissed Georgie's beautiful golden curls and tried to transmit health into her.

'Please get better. Please get better. Please get better,' I whispered, but I knew that she was very, very sick.

I walked into the surgery and asked to see the doctor immediately. The receptionist replied that he was fully booked and that I would have to come back the next day.

'I can't wait. This child is very sick. I have to see him today.'

'Well, I'm afraid, Mrs Horlick, that you will just have to wait. I'm sorry.'

'This child urgently needs a blood test. Please can you ask the doctor to arrange for one immediately.' At this point, another doctor walked into the room and asked what the problem was. I explained briefly and he took one look at Georgie and said that she looked terrible and that she should definitely have a blood test. A few minutes later, I was in a room with Georgie having her blood taken.

'What a brave little girl you have been, Georgie. Would you like a sweet?' The nurse produced a huge jar of sweets and offered it to her. Georgie shook her head and the nurse gave me a sympathetic look. She knew as well as I did. Georgie was a very sick child.

I returned home and Georgie suddenly seemed to have a burst of energy. She demanded that she should be allowed to go to school. I was somewhat doubtful about whether this was a good idea, but I decided to let her go. Tim was at home as we were both still on holiday and Joan was having a few days off. I took Alice, who was now ten months old, with me and we drove to the nursery school. It was within easy walking distance, but I did not want Georgie to get overtired. I spent an anxious two and a half hours at home hoping that she was all right at school and then jumped into the car to go and collect her. She looked fine when she came out and she was eager to tell me about everything that she had been doing, but she did want me to carry her back to the car. Just as I opened the door and started to strap her in, the car telephone rang. It was Tim. The doctor had rung and he wanted us to go immediately to a private hospital with Georgie.

'But that's a maternity hospital,' I said. It was the hospital where Georgie had been born. Tim told me that it also had a private children's ward. The irony struck me hard. The hospital where Georgie had been born might be the place where she died. I still did not know what was wrong with her, but I sensed that her life was in grave danger.

I could not locate Joan before we left for the hospital, so I rang my brother and asked him to come over to look after Alice. He had little experience of looking after children at that stage, but I knew he would cope. I rapidly packed some things for Georgie and me on the assumption that we would have to stay in the hospital for some time and Tim and I jumped into the car with her.

When we arrived, we were told that a paediatrician would see us shortly. Tim and I paced up and down the corridor whilst Georgie went to sleep in our allocated room. The minutes passed extremely slowly and no one told us what was happening, so I went to the nurse's desk and asked when we would be seeing the doctor. She said that he had been delayed but would be there within the hour. My heart sank. Having previously felt that I did not really want to know what was wrong, I was now desperate to find out.

'You must know what's wrong with Georgie,' I said to the sister. 'Can't you tell me?'

'I'm afraid you must wait for the doctor,' was the reply.

The next hour passed even more slowly than the last. Periodically I stopped pacing up and down and went into Georgie's room. She looked almost lifeless lying on the hospital bed with a completely white face and breathing very shallowly. I leaned on the bed and put my head next to hers, stroking her hair, but she did not stir.

When the doctor arrived, Tim and I were called into a small room. The doctor seemed uneasy and gave us a weak smile, introduced himself and shook our hands. There was a slight pause after we had sat down as he braced himself to tell us what was wrong with Georgie.

'We have got the results of the blood test that was done this morning,' he said, 'and I am afraid that Georgina is not very well. Her haemoglobin is 4 and a normal count would be between 10 and 13. That accounts for why she looks so pale. Platelets are the things in the blood that prevent bruising and allow scratches to heal. Her platelet count has also collapsed. A possible explanation is that she has leukaemia, but we will have to do a bone marrow test tomorrow to confirm that.'

We were both silent, taking in what we had just been told. Tim was looking at the ground and I could see that he was unable to speak, so I asked, 'When you say that a possible explanation is that she has leukaemia, how likely is it that she doesn't?'

The doctor thought for a moment and then said, 'I would say that there is a 50 per cent chance that she doesn't have leukaemia.'

'If she doesn't have leukaemia, then what is wrong with her?'

'I won't be able to answer that question until we have done more tests. We are going to do a blood transfusion now to get that haemoglobin up.' I asked a few more questions about what the bone marrow test would involve and was told that Georgie would be given a general anaesthetic and that a needle would then be inserted in her hip and a sample of bone marrow taken. 'Do you have any more questions? Mr Horlick, you've been very quiet. Is there anything that you would like to ask?' Tim shook his head, unable to say anything. I thought that the doctor had been extremely insensitive to ask that question. It was clear that Tim was upset and was trying to come to terms with what we had just been told.

We returned to the room unable to say anything to each other at first.

'Well, there is a 50 per cent chance that she doesn't have leukaemia,' I finally said.

'She's got leukaemia. He's just trying to let you down slowly.'

'They can't do that sort of thing. If it was conclusive, surely he would have told us.' I clung on to the forlorn hope that it was not leukaemia. Perhaps she was suffering from some sort of acute anaemia and the blood transfusion would do the trick.

When the blood transfusion began, Georgie began to change colour. She remained asleep throughout and I sat by her bed holding her hand. As the minutes passed, she got pinker and pinker until suddenly she looked like a normal healthy child again. She began to wake up, stretching and yawning. She sat up.

'Hello, darling,' I said, 'do you feel better?' She nodded. Maybe, I thought with desperate hope, that was all she needed.

We decided that it would be best if Tim returned to Alice that evening and so I was left alone with Georgie. We had agreed that there was no point in telling anyone about the situation until we knew exactly what was wrong with Georgie, but I needed to talk to my parents. I could tell my mother agreed with Tim that the doctor was just trying to let me down slowly. When I had put the telephone down, I bathed Georgie, put her in her pyjamas and then she went back to sleep. I had a bed next to her in her room, but I could not sleep. I kept going over and over the events of the day in my head. It had been a very long day, a day that I would never forget in my entire life. If it was leukaemia, did that mean certain death? I should have asked the doctor more questions. Why didn't I ask what the prognosis would be?

I had a sudden urge to walk up and down the corridor again and so, putting on my slippers, I went out of the room. The nurses on night duty were concerned about me and invited me to sit with them at the desk. We talked about Georgie and they told me that the prognosis for childhood leukaemia was extremely good. If that was what Georgie had, it absolutely did not mean that she was going to die imminently.

'You'll need all your strength over the next few days,' one of them said to me. 'Let me get you a sleeping tablet. You need to rest.' I had never taken a sleeping tablet before, but on that occasion I agreed. I returned to our room and fell into a deep, dreamless sleep.

The next morning, Georgie was awake before me and, as I began to emerge from the darkness, I was encouraged to see that her cheeks still had the lovely pink colour that the blood transfusion had given her. We got dressed and had breakfast together and she seemed better than she had been for weeks. Then there came a knock at the door. A man came in who introduced himself as the oncologist who would be looking after Georgie. He said that the bone marrow test would be done that afternoon and that they would put in a Hickman line at the same time. This was a tube that would give direct access to the bloodstream and allow the nurses to take blood and give drugs without putting needles into Georgie. The chemotherapy would start the next day.

'I thought that the bone marrow test was meant to establish whether Georgie has leukaemia, so why are you talking about Hickman lines and chemotherapy before you even have the result?'

'We know from the blood test that was done yesterday that she has leukaemia,' the oncologist replied. 'The bone marrow test will establish exactly what type of leukaemia it is so that we can give the most appropriate treatment. When we know which protocol Georgie is going to be on, we will discuss what is going to happen more fully with you.'

'But the paediatrician we saw last night told me that there was a 50 per cent chance that she does not have leukaemia.'

'I'm afraid, Mrs Horlick, that there is no doubt that she has leukaemia.' I felt as though my whole world was collapsing about me. I had suspected for some days that Georgie had leukaemia, but now I had a definite answer. I was shattered. Anger was building up inside me. I felt that I had been misled.

The oncologist tried to reassure me, knowing that he had just confirmed my worst fears. He said that the prognosis was reasonably good. The white count had been high, but not too high, and girls tended to do better than boys. About 65 per cent of children with the type of leukaemia that they thought Georgie had made a full recovery, he told me. When he had gone, I left Georgie playing happily on the floor of her room and went to see the sister. We had struck up a good rapport and I needed to talk to someone. She reinforced the message about the prognosis being good.

'You knew last night that she had leukaemia, didn't you?' I said. She nodded. 'Then that doctor who talked to Tim and me last night must have known too.' She nodded again. I could not possibly deal with someone who I felt had misled me. She said that it was useful to have a paediatrician in the background in these cases and I said that the one that I wanted was Jake Mackinnon, a wonderful doctor who had examined Georgie at birth and whom I had kept in touch with ever since. During the desperate months that I had spent trying to get Georgie diagnosed, I had not gone to see Jake. This was because I had rung him in a panic when Alice was a very small baby and told him that I had found lumps in her chest. He had met me at his surgery very early the next morning and told me that many baby girls got hard patches around the nipples and that it was nothing to worry about. I thought that if I went to him with Georgie and it turned out to be nothing, he would have thought that I was an idiot.

Jake loved Georgie and he was very sad when he saw her looking so frail and sick. She grinned from ear to ear when he walked through the door. It was months since she had last seen him, but she remembered him. He examined her, tickling under her arms and she was in fits of giggles. As he left, he promised to come and see us regularly and told me that if I wanted anything to read about leukaemia to let him know.

When Jake had left, I picked Georgie up in my arms and hugged her tight.

'My poor darling.' Tears began to roll down my face. 'We are going to fight and we are going to win, darling. We are going to beat this horrible disease.' She clung to me for about five minutes. She did not understand why I was upset, but she wanted to try and make her mummy feel better. 'I love you so much, darling. I love you . . .'

It is very difficult to explain illness to someone who is not yet three. Georgie was bright and spoke very well for her age, but there was no way that she could possibly take in the enormity of the news that we had been given. She had seen me crying as I rang members of the family and close friends to tell them the sad news, but this did not particularly seem to affect her. She sat watching a video or playing with her toys as I went through the story of her diagnosis over and over again.

Telling Tim's parents was the most difficult. Tim's mother had been fighting breast cancer for fifteen years and took the news very badly. She knew only too well how devastating the drugs were and how terrible Georgie was going to feel. She was so upset when Tim told her that she went for a long walk round Bath in the pouring rain to reflect on the news.

I also had to tell Leonard. I was still on holiday and he was expecting me back at work in a couple of days. He is a very family-orientated person and he was very upset when I broke the news to him. Leonard came round to see me at the hospital and brought Georgie a beautiful toy rabbit to cheer her up. He was profoundly shocked when he saw Georgie looking so ill and he found it difficult to talk to me. I tried to look jolly, but it did not improve the situation.

'Don't hurry back. Tom and I can cope. You look after Georgie,' he said. He would ring me every other day to find out how she was. 'You are looking after yourself too, aren't you? You are eating properly and sleeping?' I was really touched by his concern for us both.

Georgie was not allowed to have any lunch as she was going down to the operating theatre that afternoon. She was given a minute operating gown with teddy bears and other toys printed on it. As she sat in her bed waiting for the trolley to arrive, I took a photograph of her. She grinned at me, cheeks still aglow after the transfusion and I really could not believe that she was so sick.

'I'm hungry and I'm thirsty, Mummy!' she said crossly.

'You can't have anything until after the operation, darling.'

'But, Mummy, I'm really, really hungry.'

Eventually, the operating trolley arrived and I went down to the theatre with my little girl. Tim had returned to the hospital, but he had to stay in the room as only one of us was allowed to go down with her.

'See if you can count to ten before you fall asleep,' the anaesthetist said to Georgie.

'One, two, three, four, five, six, seven . . .' She was out.

'Thanks, Mum,' the anaesthetist said. As I walked towards the door with the nurse, my eyes filled with tears. I might never see Georgie again. She might not wake up from the anaesthetic. That fear resurfaces within me every time Georgie has an anaesthetic.

I went back to the room to wait with Tim. When I went into the room, I was surprised to see Charlie Curtis, one of our close friends and a colleague of mine.

'I had to come and see you when I heard about Georgie.' He put his arms round me and gave me a hug. 'You poor things.'

Georgie could not have been down in the operating theatre for more than three-quarters of an hour, but it seemed like an eternity. I went out once or twice to ask the sister if she was ready yet. Without any warning, the door of the room suddenly opened and Georgie was wheeled in. She was lying on the trolley, naked, with a plastic tube coming out of her chest and a foil blanket loosely wrapped round her. Charlie looked completely horrified. I explained what the tube was and found a nightie to put on her. Georgie was barely awake. 'Mummy, I want you.'

'I'm here, darling. Daddy's here too and Charlie has come to see you.'

'Hello, Georgie,' Charlie said, but her eyes were closed and she was asleep. Charlie slipped away and Tim and I were left alone with her. Tim stayed with us in the hospital that night and for a few nights afterwards, until we decided that he ought to go home to Alice. She had Joan, of course, but we were worried that she would feel insecure if she thought we had both disappeared.

The chemotherapy began with an overnight infusion and Georgie went to sleep with a drip attached to her Hickman line. The drug, daunarubicin, was bright red and looked menacing, but the doctors hoped that it would get her into remission in combination with a number of less potent drugs that would be given over the course of the first two weeks. This was called the induction block. The purpose of the chemotherapy was to destroy the white blood cells, which carry leukaemia, but they are also the cells that fight infection. During the chemotherapy, Georgie's immunity would be temporarily obliterated as well. She would have to stay in hospital throughout this process and, if she got a temperature, she would need heavy doses of intravenous antibiotics. We were told that we were likely to be in the hospital for about nine weeks.

As we had full medical insurance, we did not have to worry about the cost of Georgie's treatment, but I did want to know whether we were in the right place. Two of Georgie's godparents happened to be doctors and both of them came to see her during the many weeks that we spent in the hospital. I quizzed them about whether we should have opted for the NHS. They did not emphatically say that we should have, but they did say that as Georgie was on a national protocol which set out exactly which drugs in what doses she was to have and when, the nursing care was the most important thing. I was very impressed with the nursing care. All the nurses had been trained at London teaching hospitals and many of them were working here because it provided them with greater flexibility than the NHS. There were some who only wanted to work nights and others who wanted to work part time as they had small children. I had no doubt that the nursing care could not be much better.

Being in the private sector also meant that Georgie had her own room and I could sleep with her. If she had been on an open ward, I would have had to leave her every night. Also, private care meant that she had a Hickman line which in those days the NHS regarded as being too expensive for all patients to have.

Every day, Georgie would have a full blood count and I would look at the results to see if there was any improvement. After the chemotherapy was administered, the white count stayed down for about ten days and then began to edge up. When Georgie's counts were finally good enough, we were allowed to wander around the ward freely and go to the playroom. We were even given permission occasionally to take Georgie out of the hospital for a couple of hours. The park was nearby and there was a playground there which Georgie loved. I also took her shopping one day. She was going to be in hospital on her birthday and I wanted to buy her a new dress. She was desperate to go on a red bus and begged me to let her. I worried about the germs she might catch in such a crowded place, but I did not have the heart to refuse her. She adored her ride.

Joan brought Alice to see us every day. I missed her terribly when she was not there. If I had been at work, I would have seen less of her, but I was not at home to put her in her cot at night and to get her up in the morning. I would sit in Georgie's room and cuddle Alice, stroking her silky blonde hair, and I could feel the anguish temporarily seeping away. She would struggle slightly after a while and want to get down and crawl on the floor. Then she would pull herself up on a chair and look at me with a grin. When there was a room free, the sister would let me put Alice in it for her sleep, but if there was not, Joan would have to take her home early, otherwise she would get ratty and cry.

Every evening I would watch television and do my embroidery. I have never been very good at just sitting in front of the television. I have to have something else to do at the same time. I thought that if I did the embroidery, I could either have it framed for Georgie when it was finished or have it made into a cushion cover for her room. As I watched the television, the collapse of the Berlin Wall was happening. The reports showed hundreds of people streaming across the border from East Germany to West Germany and people celebrating in the streets. Tears poured down my face.

Much of my time was spent reading as I wanted to find out as much as I could about leukaemia. I took Jake up on his offer and he brought me a pile of articles from the *Lancet*, the leading medical journal. I spent hours trying to understand them, but most of them were beyond me. I did pick up some very useful information though. One article detailed a study showing that patients treated in centres where there were a large number of patients being treated with the same disease did significantly better than patients treated as one-off cases or in small groups. This seemed pretty logical to me. A true centre of excellence where there were a number of real experts working as a team was likely to achieve better results.

I began to wonder again whether we were in the best place. As I looked around the ward, there were no other British children there with leukaemia. Most of the patients were from countries which could not offer treatment for cancer on a par with the UK and their embassies were paying for them to be there. Tim and I talked about whether we should consider moving to the NHS and we decided that we would revisit this when the main part of the treatment was over.

We still had the radiotherapy to get through and that was the worst part of the treatment. I was told that, as it was only to be given to Georgie's head, there would be little in the way of side-effects. However, it was inevitable that some brain cells would be killed and brain cells, I was told, were the only cells in the body that did not regenerate. We were warned that Georgie's growth might be affected and that we should look out for learning difficulties as she got older.

I was horrified and talked to Jake Mackinnon at once. He tried to reassure me, saying that Georgie was so bright that it would not make any difference to her academic ability. What he told me was of some comfort, but I could not bear the thought of her brain cells being destroyed for ever and I had an irrational fear that she would not recognize me after she had had the first dose. I was told by the haematologist that cranial irradiation had been a major breakthrough in the treatment of leukaemia and that relapse rates had declined dramatically when it was introduced into the protocol. It seemed that there was no choice. All I could do was have Georgie educationally assessed before the treatment started. If I knew what her strengths and weaknesses were before the radiotherapy, I could look out for problems later. The educational psychologist agreed with Jake. She thought that Georgie could afford to lose a few brain cells.

Georgie was to have ten doses of radiotherapy over two weeks at St Bartholomew's Hospital in the City. It was nine weeks since Georgie had been diagnosed and we had been in the hospital for the whole of this time. I was very relieved when I was told that she would be allowed to return home and go to Barts as an outpatient. I decided that I would go to work in the morning and then arrange for the radiotherapy to be done in the early afternoon. Although Leonard had been insistent that I should take as much time off as I needed, I felt a real desire to go into the office to see everyone and make sure that everything was under control. Joan would drive to my office with Georgie and Alice at lunch-time, I would run down to meet them and drive them all over to the hospital. Before the treatment was due to start, however, Georgie had to have a mask made to fit her face. She was given an anaesthetic and a technician took an imprint of her face using some sort of plaster from which a perspex mask was made. I asked what the mask was for and was told that it would be put over Georgie's face and then screwed down into the table so that her head could not move.

We arrived at Barts for the first dose of radiotherapy and were required to see the doctor first. There was a long queue of people standing outside the door. Each one went in and was out again two minutes later. It was soon our turn.

'Is she well? No infections? Okay. I'll see you downstairs in a few minutes.'

When we got downstairs, we were shown into the treatment room. A nurse, holding Georgie's mask, asked her to lie on the table that was under the enormous machine which was to zap her. I lifted Georgie up and she lay down. She did not seem at all worried. I was petrified. I was still sure that she would not recognize me when she had had the treatment; that she would be changed for ever. The table had no sides and was very narrow.

'Surely this isn't safe,' I said. 'If she falls off, she'll break her neck.'

'She won't fall off,' said the nurse as she placed the mask

over Georgie's face and screwed it to the table. She patted Georgie on the arm and then put on a music tape for her to listen to. The consultant came in and checked that everything was all right and then we all left the room. I expected Georgie to cry or ask me to stay, but she did not. Instead, she started to sing along very loudly to the tape and we could hear it over a loudspeaker outside the room. The nurse smiled. I could not understand how she could be so cheerful when something so awful was about to happen to her. The machine began to move over her head and Georgie continued to sing at the top of her voice.

When it was all over, I rushed into the room. Georgie did recognize me. She seemed just the same and she was just as happy as when we had gone into the room. I was overcome with relief.

I was not expected back in the office that afternoon, so I drove Georgie, Alice and Joan home from the hospital. We had been in the car for less than ten minutes when Georgie's mood suddenly changed. She began to whimper. 'I'm going to be sick, Mummy. I'm going to be sick.' She was violently sick all over herself and the car. 'My head hurts, Mummy.' I put Georgie straight to bed when we got home and cuddled her. I did not want to let her go. She fell into a deep sleep and I lay next to her wondering how she would feel after ten doses. She had been such a brave little girl. As she lay in our bed, she looked so small. Her golden curls were gone and she looked as white as the pillowcase. I loved her so much. I could not bear the thought of losing her. Everyone kept saying that she would be fine, but it was difficult to believe as I lay there with her in my arms.

The next day, we went back for the second dose. I told the doctor what had happened and he claimed that it had not been caused by the radiotherapy.

'Is she on any medication?' he asked. She was taking one drug. 'It must be that,' he said.

Georgie was just as bad after the second dose of radio-therapy. She was sick twice in the car on the way home and tears were streaming down her face. I rang the haematologist the moment we got home, but could not get hold of him. I wanted to ask him if Georgie could stop taking the drug while she was having the radiotherapy. I had a friend who was a haematologist so I turned to her for advice. She said that it was the combination of the drug and the radiotherapy that was making Georgie sick and that it was not essential for her to take the drug over those few days. She recommended that we should stop it. I finally got through to Georgie's haematologist and he agreed that the drug could be stopped. The moment that Georgie stopped taking the drug, she stopped being sick.

There was still a question mark over whether Georgie was going to have the third block of chemotherapy. Things were brought to a head over Christmas when she became very ill with an infection. We were staying in Cheshire with my parents and Georgie was admitted to the local NHS hospital. The doctor who saw us said that it would be better if we went back to London and saw our own doctors, so I jumped in the car and set off for the hospital. It turned out that the infection was in her Hickman line. We were told that it would have to be removed and that this would mean that Georgie would definitely not be having the final block of treatment.

When I next saw the haematologist, I quizzed him about why he had decided that it would not be necessary to give the final block of chemotherapy. He said that he had spoken to a number of other leukaemia experts and explained the details of Georgie's case. They had all agreed that it would not be necessary for her to have the final block. This disturbed me as I had read in one of the *Lancet* articles that Jake had given me that the experts were beginning to think that children with leukaemia should have as much chemotherapy as possible.

We moved into the maintenance phase of the treatment which we were told would last for about two years. This would involve having a lumbar puncture once a month together with an injection of a drug called vincristine. Between times, Georgie would take oral chemotherapy drugs. The dose would be varied according to her blood count and it would be necessary to have a blood test every two weeks. I had read a little about this part of the treatment and asked a few questions which I already knew the answers to. I did not get satisfactory replies and this added to my concern. The question that lingered in my mind was whether Georgie's chances of being cured had been reduced as a result of not having the final block of treatment? I went to see Jake Mackinnon in a barely controlled panic. He said that there was no reason why

Georgie could not move to an NHS hospital if that was what Tim and I wanted. I mentioned Great Ormond Street and he agreed that this would be the best place to go, but he warned that it was heavily oversubscribed.

I had just started to get involved with the Leukaemia Research Fund and was due to attend one of their functions that evening. I met Gordon Pillar, the founder of the fund, and told him about Georgie's illness. He insisted that I ring Professor Judith Chessells at Great Ormond Street first thing in the morning. He would tell her that I was going to call. I could not sleep that night. As I tossed and turned, I could see the expression on his face in my mind's eye when I told him about Georgie. His reaction had made me feel even more concerned about her.

When I took Georgie to see Professor Chessells, she expressed complete dismay that Georgie had been treated at a private hosptial.

'Did the doctors tell you what protocol she was on?'

'Well, they told me that she was on UKALL X D, but they didn't do the final block of chemo.'

She sighed and shook her head. 'Before I make any judgement on whether she has had the appropriate treatment, I need to see the notes. I will get in touch with the hospital and ask them to send me copies. In the meantime, she should keep taking the oral drugs. Come back and see me in two weeks. I should have the notes by then.'

By going privately, we thought we were giving Georgie the best but now I was beginning to worry that we had not. If we had not had medical insurance, the choice would have been made for us and Georgie would have started off at one of the centres of excellence for paediatric oncology in London. There was clear evidence, which I had read about in medical journals, that children treated in these centres had a better chance of being cured.

When Professor Chessells got the notes from the private hospital, she rang to reassure me that it looked as though Georgie had had appropriate treatment. It would have been better if she had had the final block of chemotherapy, but she was not in the high-risk category. She was a girl and her white count had not been too high when she was diagnosed and so Professor Chessells felt that we should continue with maintenance. Tim and I were so relieved. We would not know for many years whether Georgie had been cured, but at least she had been given the right treatment. I thought that I had probably overreacted and had been slightly paranoid, but I was pleased that we were at Great Ormond Street. I felt happier that Georgie was now being treated with so many other children with the same disease and I found it comforting to share our experiences with other mothers when we went to the clinic each month.

As we moved on from the immediate period of crisis, Tim and I both began to realize that it was important that we did not allow Georgie's illness to become all consuming. We had Alice to consider and a third child on the way. I had had a desperate urge to get pregnant when Georgie first became ill and, shortly after we moved her to Great Ormond Street, I discovered that I was. We had to assume that Georgie was going to get better and we did not want her to become spoilt by being treated differently from the others.

It is extremely difficult to treat a very sick child normally. We were tempted when Georgie did not want to do something to say that it was not important and let her off. We had to be careful not to over-indulge her. When you have a child with a potentially fatal disease, the thought that she might not survive always lurks at the back of your mind. You want her lasting memory of you to be as kind and loving parents, not mean taskmasters denying her wishes. But we had to assume that Georgie would reach adulthood, as the majority of children with leukaemia do these days, and what would she do when there were no doting parents to hang on her every word? We resolved that whatever the future held, we would try to live as normal a life as possible as a family.

When Georgie first became ill, my immediate reaction was to give up work, but Tim urged me to wait and see what life was like once we were back home. Georgie went back to school with great enthusiasm and it didn't matter to her that she did not have any hair. I used to put a hat on her when we went out and she would pull it off within seconds.

'Put it back on! Your head will get cold,' I would say. After all, it was February, but she did not care. The children at school were too young to tease her. They accepted her as she was and she slipped back into her normal routine without any problems.

I returned to work. I found that the demands on me at

work meant that I had little time to worry about Georgie. Our monthly visit to the hospital became the focal point for that. I would have butterflies in my stomach as I waited for her blood result to come through and then would be overcome with relief when I saw that it was normal. When we left Great Ormond Street, I would put the worrying to the back of my mind for another month. Looking back, I am pleased that I listened to Tim. It was better for all of us that Georgie and I were so busy.

Leonard was delighted that I had returned. I explained to him that if Georgie got an infection when her blood counts were low, she would be admitted to hospital for a week and I would have to go with her. I would also have to spend at least half a day each month at Great Ormond Street Hospital. He was very supportive and said that he understood this. Carol had been very kind to me throughout Georgie's illness. She too had come to visit me in the hospital and she had rung me regularly to find out how things were. Leonard and I agreed that I would play it by ear and see if I could cope with the job and a sick child. Since he seemed to be in such a good mood, I broke the news to him that I was pregnant.

seven

Serena, my third child, was born in November 1990. It was a quick and easy birth and I was allowed to go home twenty-four hours after she arrived. A few days after she was born, Tim's father rang me to tell me that my mother-in-law, who had fought a long and hard battle against cancer, had been told that it had got into her liver and that she only had weeks to live. She did not want to die in a hospice and he was determined to look after her. We all rallied round and visited Bath frequently during those difficult weeks. At least my mother-in-law was able to see Serena before she died.

Whilst I was on maternity leave, a couple of members of my team, Charlie Curtis and James Goulding, told me that they were thinking of leaving. The asset management division had continued to grow strongly and Warburgs had floated it on the stock exchange and renamed it Mercury Asset Management (MAM). Warburgs retained a 75 per cent interest in MAM, but we were in a separate building again and had very little to do with the bank. Charlie and James took the view that the business was now so big that it would be difficult for it to grow as quickly as it had done in the past. They had been looking for opportunities and had decided that Morgan Grenfell was an interesting prospect. It had been one of the leading players in the UK pension fund business, but it had lost many clients as a result of poor performance. From the outside, it seemed that this was due to the fact that their international fund management business had grown strongly and that they had moved a number of talented people from the UK business into it. Charlie had identified Morgan Grenfell as a possible recovery situation because Keith Percy had recently joined from a very successful firm called PDFM. Under his leadership, PDFM had grown strongly over the eighties having been in some difficulty when he first went there.

I had just had a baby and Georgie was still on treatment, so I was not at all enthusiastic when they mentioned this idea to me. Charlie decided to go ahead and meet Keith in order to assess how interesting Morgan Grenfell was. I was still on maternity leave, but had to go to an important client meeting with him one day. I left Serena with Joan and drove to Bloomsbury where the meeting was. I was trying to concentrate on what I was going to say to the trustees, but Charlie could not stop talking about Morgan Grenfell. He was brimming over with excitement and urged me to meet Keith. Charlie is a very good fund manager with an excellent instinct for undervalued shares. He was approaching this in the same way and was certain that he was on to a winner.

I was going skiing for a week and did not have time to make contact with Keith before I went. Whilst Tim and I were in France, I thought about whether it was really viable for me to leave MAM. Charlie and James thought we needed a new challenge. I was inclined to agree. I had achieved as much as I could at MAM and the senior management were very young and unlikely to move aside to let people like me and John Richards try our hand at running the overall business. If I wanted more management responsibility, I would have to move.

I liked Keith the moment that we met. He came across as being very straightforward and charming. As I discussed with him what needed to be done to revive the UK pension fund business at Morgan Grenfell, it became clear that we had very much the same outlook on life. He had known little about me before we met, but he had clearly done his homework. He was impressed with what we had achieved at MAM and indicated that he would like to take the discussions forward. I was itching to try my hand at turning the business around, but I still was not sure that I wanted to leave MAM. I had been there for eight years and had been promoted very rapidly to be made a director just six months before. The main reason that I was prevaricating about leaving, though, was that I was worried about how Leonard would take my departure. I knew that I could not live in his shadow for ever and if I was going to stay at MAM, I should really ask for a new challenge, but I thought that he would be insulted if I asked to work in another part of the organization.

Keith was very keen that the existing Morgan Grenfell team should buy into the idea of Charlie, James and I joining, and we had many meetings where we discussed our ideas for improving the business with them. Many of them were very straightforward. From what we had been told, Morgan Grenfell lacked some basic business disciplines which we felt were essential for it to become a leading force in pension fund management again. We all felt that we could work with the existing team and I realized that the time was fast approaching when I would have to make my choice. Keith knew that I had three children, but he regarded this as being irrelevant. I told him about Georgie's illness and explained that I might have to disappear to the hospital with her occasionally, but he did not regard this as an issue. Keith made me a formal offer the day before Tim and I were due to go to Venice to celebrate his thirtieth birthday. I asked if he would mind if I thought about it whilst I was away and he agreed.

Tim and I had not dared to go abroad since Georgie fell ill as we were worried that she would get an infection when we were not there. As she had been well for so long, I decided that we would risk it. After all we had been through, Tim and I needed some time alone together. The weather in Venice was wonderful. There were blue skies every day and, as it was June, it was not too hot. I had bought an excellent guidebook and I planned routes for us to follow each day. We explored the whole city during the week we were there.

One day, we returned to the hotel exhausted and ready for an early night and found an urgent message telling us to ring St George's Hospital. Georgie had chicken pox, which can be extremely dangerous for immuno-suppressed children. I spoke to Joan and said that I would try to get back as quickly as I could. She told me to stay in Venice. My mother had taken the other two children and Georgie was being given acyclovir, a drug that helped to reduce the impact of chicken pox, and the doctors did not think it was a bad case at all. None the less, I rang the airport to see if there were any seats on the flights to Heathrow the next day. All the planes were full. I spoke to my mother and she urged me to stay put. In the end, I did.

As our week in Venice drew to an end, I talked to Tim about my job. He said that it would be a major risk to go to Morgan Grenfell, but as Keith Percy was already there and Charlie and James were going with me, we would have a reasonable chance of turning the business round. He thought that I had got into a rut at MAM and that it would do me good to have a change. He had already had three jobs since we had left Oxford whereas I had only had one. He was an expert on making such decisions compared to me and I trusted his judgement. Now that I had decided that I was going to leave, I wanted to get my resignation over and done with as soon as possible, so I rang Leonard's secretary and enquired if he was going to be in the office the next day. I was told that he would be and so I decided to go straight to the City from the airport to resign.

'What are you doing here?' Leonard asked.

'I had one or two things to do,' I bluffed.

'Nice time in Venice?'

'Lovely, thanks.' I moved a few papers round my desk and then asked if I could speak to him in a meeting room. Leonard was not expecting me to resign. That was evident from the look of shock on his face when I handed him the letter that I had written. There was an awkward silence.

'I need a new challenge. It's time to move on,' I said uncertainly.

'I can tear this up and we can forget all about it,' he said.

'No, I'm going to Morgan Grenfell, Leonard.'

'It's a shame. We made a great team.'

'I know. I owe you everything . . .'

'Don't!' he said, putting his hand up. I dashed out of the room. I had to leave the building otherwise I knew I would start to cry in front of everyone.

When Leonard found out that Charlie and James were coming with me, his sadness turned to anger. I spent the weekend in the hospital with Georgie and barely thought about the situation. Georgie was allowed home on the Sunday and that evening, Leonard rang me. He was very matter-of-fact and said that I should go into the office the next day to hand over my security pass and my American Express card. The personnel director would deal with it. I was racked with guilt. After I had put the telephone down, I got some writing paper and started to write another letter to Leonard. I wanted him to know how grateful I was to him for all that he had done for me during my time at MAM.

Keith had made it clear during our many meetings that he believed I needed to spend some time on the shop floor before I could take over the management of the business. I thought long and hard about this and in the end decided that he was right. People do not like having new bosses imposed on them from outside. I had to spend some time as an ordinary fund manager in order to really get to know the existing members of the team. Keith said that he believed that the existing management would welcome my input on how the investment process and the general running of the business could be improved. My former colleagues at MAM found it difficult to understand my move. It looked to them like a step down rather than up.

I was on eight weeks' notice under my contract with MAM. They did not want me in the office as I was going to a competitor and so I had to stay at home. I was still being paid by MAM and could not do anything that could have been construed as working for my new firm. I did have time to think about the task ahead, however, and how I was going to tackle it. I had never worked in a manufacturing business, but I had analysed many as part of my job as an investment manager. I suspected that the key elements in turning any business around were the same. Manufacturing businesses may have buildings and machines to manage, but the people are pretty important too. I was convinced that the success of any business depended on having the right people and motivating them properly.

As I thought more about this, I decided that motivation was not just about money. It was about creating an environment in which people enjoyed working. When I joined Morgan Grenfell, my aim would be to get the best out of people whether they were young or old, experienced fund managers or less experienced. I realized there would be some individuals who, given a chance, would expend

large amounts of energy on internal politics. In any organization there are always people who are dissatisfied with
their lot and can quite happily spend their days moaning
about how the organization undervalues them. I knew that
weak leadership would allow these types of people to
dominate the office environment and, if this happened, we
would not succeed in turning the business around.

MAM had been successful because there was strong
leadership and this was what Morgan Grenfell needed if it
was going to improve. This did not mean autocratic
leadership as far as I was concerned. It meant setting out a
vision of where the organization was going and getting the
team to buy into it. It meant getting to know the individuals involved in the business and giving them an
opportunity to express their views as to how we could move
forward. Many organizations have a belief that everything
and anything that is being discussed at top management
level is secret. In the majority of cases, this stems from the
need of top management to feel that it is completely in
control. It is also a way for it to differentiate itself from the
next layer of management. The next layer may, however,
have interesting ideas and they are usually nearer to the
actual business and understand the needs of clients and
customers better. I knew that it would be a great mistake
not to take account of the views of those lower down the
hierarchy.

As a graduate trainee at Warburgs in the mid-eighties, I
was invited to attend a meeting with some of the senior
fund managers and Lord Hanson, probably Britain's lead-

ing industrialist at that time. He had started with a small company and had made a number of high-profile takeovers of leading companies which had all previously performed badly over a long period. He had restructured them and built his company, Hanson Trust, into one of the largest on the stock exchange. I had written the briefing note and Carol Galley, who was in charge of the UK institutional business, encouraged me to ask questions. Lord Hanson was at the pinnacle of his success and I listened in awe to his exposition of how he had built his company. I asked him if, when he acquired companies, he had to recruit heavily. He said that in every acquisition he had made, he had been amazed by how much talent there was below the top layer of management. There were always young, enthusiastic people with bright ideas as to how the business could be better managed. Perhaps the management of those companies that Lord Hanson acquired would have kept their independence if they had listened to some of those ideas.

I arrived at Morgan Grenfell with a clear vision of what I thought needed to be done to improve the business but without the authority to bring about real change. Some of my ideas were adopted by the senior members of the team and change did occur, but not enough change. In investment management, performance is the key to whether a business will prosper or not. If the UK stock market goes up by 10 per cent and your funds only go up by 9 per cent, no one will want to give you their money to manage. You can only be successful if you outperform the index consistently. If a fund manager outperforms by a small amount each year, this will accumulate into a significant added return over time.

After Charlie, James and I arrived, Morgan Grenfell's performance continued to be lacklustre and its long-term record was poor. A number of pension funds had taken their money away and further sackings were announced after we arrived. I was becoming deeply frustrated. I knew what needed to be done to stem the loss of business, but I did not have the authority to do it. I often talked to Keith about this, but he was anxious not to upset the old team by promoting me too soon. Eventually, I became so depressed that I started to think about returning to MAM. The situation was brought to a head when Leonard unexpectedly resigned. He had spent his entire working life at MAM and I was incredulous when I heard the news. He was going to a small fund management firm called Jupiter. I spoke to John Richards and eventually to Carol Galley and Stephen Zimmerman about returning to run my old team.

On a personal level, Keith and I got on very well and I told him that I was thinking of returning to MAM. Morgan Grenfell had a number of large businesses other than the UK pension fund business and he knew that he could not commit the time that it would need to sort it out once and for all. He realized that he needed me. This spurred him into action and, almost a year to the day after I had joined, I was given the authority that I needed to sort out the business. My new title was Managing Director of Morgan Grenfell Investment Management (the company responsible for managing UK pension funds).

Once I actually had the title, I felt rather daunted by the task ahead of me. My first priority was to stop further clients removing business from us and so I began by personally visiting as many clients as I could to tell them what I intended to do in broad terms and ask for their patience. The largest pension funds tended to be the worst performing and so Keith Percy took over as the director in charge while I personally took on the management of the UK equities for those accounts. Having bought extra time, I had to make sure that the performance improved.

Professional fund managers have an enormous advantage over private investors. Major companies pay frequent visits to their offices to explain how their businesses are doing and what their strategy is for the future. When I joined Morgan Grenfell, I was insistent that the fund managers should prepare properly for these meetings. Keith Percy had already set a format of pre-meets and reports of meetings being given at the daily meeting held first thing each morning. However, the briefing notes were not in a standard format and were superficial. As Lord Hanson had pointed out, all businesses generally have talented individuals below the top level of management and Morgan Grenfell was no exception. I was delighted to find that the majority of the team was very talented and desperate for the business to succeed. Some were sceptical about the changes that I was seeking to bring about, but as they began to bear fruit, they took them up with enthusiasm and a new culture of professionalism began to establish itself. I wanted the members of my team to feel proud that they worked for Morgan Grenfell Investment Management.

I pointed out that all the companies that came to see us also had pension funds. There was, therefore, a hidden benefit in being totally professional at meetings and asking aincisive questions. Most finance directors of companies were generally consulted when a new pension fund manager was being sought and, if they were impressed by us at meetings, they would be more inclined to put us forward on such occasions. The first priority remained obtaining the most information that we could at meetings. Many companies arrived with prepared presentations and we politely told them that we would rather go straight into questions. As I showed the senior management of some of Britain's most successful companies out, I was extremely gratified when I was told that they had seldom attended meetings where the fund managers were so well informed about their company.

Occasionally we could not escape the formal presentation. I will never forget when, at a lunch in our offices, the chief executive of a major British company insisted on giving us a slide show. He refused to sit at the table and eat, but instead stood solemnly next to the screen. He tripped over the projector wires twice and bumped into the serving staff a couple of times. I had to try not to look at my colleagues as I knew that I would start to giggle. The whole event was a lesson in how not to conduct a meeting with a shareholder.

The quality of the briefing notes improved beyond belief. A spirit of competition developed too. When I had arrived, there was a research team and a fund management team. I strongly believed that there should be just one team and that all its members should do research and manage funds. Everyone became an analyst and a fund manager and was given a specific sector of the market to follow. The ex-analysts were very keen to show that they could write the best briefing notes whilst the fund managers had to demonstrate that they could remember how to write. The second page of each note contained a detailed cashflow analysis in our own format and many of the fund managers found this a real challenge. I have to say that, on balance, the analysts won, but this was primarily because the bright young graduates generally began their careers in the research team. The fund managers, however, tended to dominate the actual meetings.

A target was set for each sector by a committee of five people and this gave us a framework to work within and meant that all our funds looked similar. There was no requirement for the fund managers to buy the stocks that the analyst was recommending, but it tended to happen that way. If the analyst had clearly done all the work and had put forward a well-reasoned argument for buying each stock, it was likely that the others would follow his recommendations. There is always a tendency with this sort of system for analysts to fall in love with their sectors and have too much exposure to their favourite companies in their portfolios, but setting a target for each sector ensured that this did not happen.

As the team began to become more cohesive and better informed, the performance turned. Some members of the original research team left as they did not want to manage money and I went about recruiting to replace them. With the help of my senior colleagues, we persuaded some exceptional individuals to join us. The number of funds that each manager had was low relative to the industry average, but I convinced Keith Percy that it was a worthwhile investment in our future and that I needed the people to achieve total research coverage. Many fund management companies make the mistake of not thinking ahead. Success seems almost to take them by surprise. Good performance leads to new clients joining en masse. If enough fund managers have not been recruited ahead of time, the result is that they become overstretched. Panic sets in and they end up recruiting the wrong people. Recruiting ahead of time may increase the cost base, but when the new business does begin to flow, the fees go straight down to the bottom line. It is what fund managers describe as 'operational gearing'.

A truly successful business needs solid foundations. There are certain business disciplines that I believe should run through all organizations. Well-trained secretaries and receptionists are essential. They are the first point of contact for existing and potential customers and clients. Standard letter and internal note formats are also important. If the client flips through the file relating to your organization and sees several different letter formats, it makes a poor impression.

Having information at your fingertips about your clients is also important. There were no proper client files kept on the fund management floor when I arrived at Morgan Grenfell. Each fund manager claimed that there were up-to-date files in their desks, but when I looked at them, I was unimpressed. There was a large degree of resistance when I centralized the files and placed them in cabinets down the centre of our open-plan offices. If the fund manager was out at a meeting and a client rang, it meant that another fund manager could easily deal with the query and get at any relevant correspondence.

The most important tool that was introduced at Morgan Grenfell was the management mail system. Each incoming letter, outgoing letter, internal memorandum and note of a telephone conversation was photocopied and bound into a document which was then distributed to everyone. This allowed me to monitor exactly what was going on in the business and the quality of our service to our clients. Its existence made it less likely that a fund manager would leave a letter unanswered for long as they knew that it would be picked up by senior management if they failed to respond quickly. As the business grew, this was the best way for me to retain a total grip on it. I got used to skimming through it and it was easy to spot which were the important letters and which were routine. In my view, all organizations should have a management mail system.

As Morgan Grenfell's performance figures began to improve, the focus changed to marketing. One can never get away from the fact that the investment process is all-important in a fund management business, but there will always be other organizations with performance that is just as good. When pension funds decide to change their fund managers, they select a number of organizations that they would like to see. Some start with a long list, visit six to eight fund managers and then invite three or four to attend the final beauty parade. Others select the final three or four on the basis of written submissions alone. There is very little that one can say that is radically different about how one actually manages pension fund assets relative to the competition. It is not a particularly glamorous subject. I was determined to think of ways of making our product sound more exciting. Having done my research on who might help us, I alighted on a firm of design consultants who had a reputation for innovation.

The process began with a colleague and I making a stand-up presentation to our design team so that they could understand our business and hence help us more effectively. The brief was to simplify the messages we were trying to convey and produce visual images which would make a real impact on our potential clients. The most important thing was that this should be backed up with simple software that our marketing team could be trained to use.

After six months of work, we ended up with a presentation that we believed was miles ahead of our competitors'. One of my colleagues came up with the idea of making the booklets A5 which was half the size of everyone else's booklets. The design consultants loved this idea and so did the potential clients who we tested it on. Every time I handed out the booklets at a presentation, the trustees commented on their size and I am sure that this simple device made us more memorable. I also decided to include photographs of all the people likely to be involved with a new fund in the document so that when the trustees were reviewing what each manager had said they could remember what we looked like.

I was not content with the booklet alone. I felt that if a trustee had to sit through a number of long presentations in a day, he needed something slightly different to the norm. The design company and I therefore worked on producing some lightweight boards that could be placed on an easel. I felt that standing up and presenting with the boards would be more interesting. The boards had an advantage over slides in that you did not have to darken the room which usually had the effect of sending people off to sleep, especially if it was just after lunch. As we normally presented to between ten and fifteen people, I thought that the boards needed to be large so that everyone could see them.

The first presentation that we did with the boards was to a local authority in the North of England. The team was Keith Percy, me and William Francklin, an overseas fund manager. If we won the fund, Keith would be in charge of the overall relationship, I would buy and sell the UK shares and William would be responsible for buying and selling shares in international markets. We were due to present quite early in the morning, so we decided that we would go up the evening before and stay in a hotel near the council offices. Keith was not at all sure about the boards and would have been delighted if I had managed to lose them on the way. That was not to be.

After a rather unappetizing dinner, Keith suggested that we should have a rehearsal. We returned to his room which was minute. The other two rooms were no bigger. I put up the fold-away easel and placed the introductory board on it. Keith was going to be speaking to the first few boards and so he began. He picked up the second board and removed the other; as he did so, one crashed into a wall of the room and the other into another. William and I started to giggle.

'It'll be fine when we're in a bigger room,' I said.

After breakfast the next day, we made our way to the council offices. We could have walked, but we were not sure where we were going and it seemed easier to take a taxi. The special case for the boards only just fitted into the car. We were put in a room to wait and eventually we were invited in to begin our presentation. The members of the council who made up the investment committee looked rather puzzled as I started to pull the boards out of the case and carefully balanced them against chairs. I could see that Keith was also rather uncomfortable with the whole idea, but it was too late. We could not abandon the boards now.

It was quite clear that the boards were a distraction and that our audience was not really listening to a word that we were saying. Needless to say we did not win the contract, but I insisted on taking the boards with me to the next presentation I was due to do. I had spent a great deal of time with the design consultants creating them and I was determined to try and make them work. Keith was adamant that the A5 booklet was sufficient. At the next presentation, the audience was less understanding. Unfortunately, I failed to check how big the room was before we arrived. Not only was it a small room, but there were twelve people packed into it. I set up the easel and it was virtually impossible to manoeuvre the boards on and off it in such a small space.

As the presentation continued, my colleague and I struggled with the wretched boards and the trustees looked more and more unimpressed. After that I abandoned the boards and just stuck with the A5 booklet.

However good the materials, you cannot win a new account if the presentation is poor. All the fund managers were sent on presentation courses and Keith Percy and I used to do mock presentations so that our colleagues could hear how we wanted the important messages to be conveyed. We had reached the point where our presentations impressed most potential clients, but we did not have the long-term performance record to ensure success. Within eighteen months, the performance record had picked up considerably and we began to win new accounts. In 1993, we exceeded our new business budget by four times. In 1994, 1995 and 1996, the same thing would happen.

Real teamwork had got us to that point and this differentiated us from our competitors. Outsiders used to tell me that they could see that our team was very cohesive and they attributed our increasing success to this. The research output remained of a very high standard and the investment decisions reflected this. There was a clear Morgan Grenfell way of doing things in the UK pension fund business. When I was recruiting, I spent a great deal of time explaining what that involved and only if the potential recruit clearly bought into our way of doing things was he or she invited to join. I was not interested in people who wanted to try to reinvent what we had.

A business cannot stand still, however. It has to be

dynamic. The world around us changes all the time and there can be no holy cows. I spent a great deal of time talking to my colleagues individually about how things might be improved and, at the quarterly team lunches which I held, if someone came up with an idea and it needed investigation, I told them to go and do it.

One of my younger colleagues who had a brilliant mind was critical of the way that asset allocation (the process that results in money being divided between the different markets) was being done, so I secured a place for him on the relevant committee. Another of my colleagues was convinced that we could improve the way in which we negotiated fees for new clients and so I gave him the job of doing so. This proved to be an excellent idea of his. By taking the negotiation of fees out of the hands of those who had done the original presentation, it could be carried out more dispassionately. In other words, the negotiator was less likely to give in and reduce fees.

Four and a half years after radical changes were implemented, Morgan Grenfell had gone from being one of the worst-performing pension fund managers to the best-performing major house over one, three and five years. Many of the key players remained the same as when Keith and I had arrived at the firm and yet that seemed hard to believe given the way the business had turned around. Here was proof that a clear strategy and good business disciplines were vital to success.

Keith had said when we first met that it made no difference to him that I had children. I had demonstrated that I could raise children and pursue a career, and, now that the business was operating smoothly, I was able to go home at a reasonable time and see the children. When I had first taken on the task of sorting out the business, there had been weeks when I had hardly seen them, and Georgie would make it clear that they were not impressed. I promised her that this would be short-lived and it was. Some of the older members of the team did find it a little difficult to adjust to working with me, but that was probably more to do with my age. For a man approaching fifty to accept any thirty-one-year-old as his boss must be hard. I suspect that one or two of the wives did not like it, but I have no particular proof. It was just an impression I gained when talking to them at company events.

One thing that I did find hard to cope with was the press interest in me. Newspapers love writing articles about successful women. Endless pieces have been written over the past five years where the same boring details have been regurgitated about me: where I was educated; how old I am; how many children I have; inaccurate guesses about how much I was earning. The tone of the articles was always the same. How can this be possible? Why should it not be possible has always been my retort to that.

I was always shocked by the response of my male colleagues to this unsolicited publicity. They showed anger and threw accusing looks at me across the morning meeting table each time such an article appeared. Journalists are very unoriginal. Every time a 'successful woman' article was written, it inspired a flurry of other articles. At one point, the group personnel director told me that there was a suspicion in the upper echelons of the bank that I had employed my own PR adviser to promote myself. I was totally amazed by this accusation. I asked him how anyone could possibly think such a thing and he replied that no one could believe that I could get so much coverage without one.

Whenever a journalist rang and asked for an interview, they usually got my secretary on 'auto-pilot' saying that I was not available. One day I picked up the telephone and it was a journalist from the *Sunday Times* magazine.

'I am doing an article on successful women in the City. I want to profile three individuals and I was wondering whether you would be willing to participate.'

'Why should I want to participate?' I asked her. 'What good would it do me? I think it's wrong that you only want to write about me because I'm a woman. Pursuing women like this will only hinder our progress.'

'Are you sure that I cannot persuade you to take part?'

'I'm certain. Goodbye.' She was not interested in my point of view. All she wanted was to fill the pages of the magazine.

As I became more confident in my role as the manager of my business, I began to wonder why there were so few women in top jobs. Taking a step back and trying to analyse objectively the differences between male managers and female managers, I felt that female managers tended to be better organized than men and paid more attention to detail. They were also better man-managers. They were more interested in their colleagues as people and were more willing to listen to their problems and discuss their hopes and aspirations. I had observed that many men in top jobs had egos that got in the way of all else.

There was a new generation of university-educated women entering the City, but I began to realize that a good education was not sufficient to gain recognition and promotion. The explanation for the lack of female representation at the top of companies could only be that there were not enough men in senior positions who were prepared to give young women the break that they needed. I was extremely lucky that my first two bosses were people who believed in me as a person and felt that gender was totally irrelevant. As I wanted to have children and indeed did have them when I was relatively young, I had to accept that I was not the same as my male colleagues. I could not miss a school function and I could not delegate the care of my sick child to anyone. I had to take time off when I had another baby. Keith was prepared to accept this because he thought that I was good at my job. As far as he was concerned, this was all that counted, but I began to realize he was unusual in his thinking.

Georgie had come off her treatment completely shortly after I had joined Morgan Grenfell and had been extremely well ever since. I had stopped worrying between hospital visits and soon the time between check-ups lengthened from one month to two months. In the back of mind I kept wondering if my other two children were bone marrow matches for Georgie. I knew that if she was ever unlucky enough to relapse, it might be necessary to do a bone marrow transplant. I had picked up from some of the other mothers at Great Ormond Street that there was a one in four chance of a sibling being a match. Although mathematically the same odds applied to each child, I was tempted to have a fourth child. There had to be a better chance of a match if Georgie had three siblings rather than two. Tim and I felt that three was not a good number anyway. They were always fighting which I put down to them all being the same sex. I knew other families of three where there were boys and girls and they did not seem to have quite as much conflict. I had warned Keith when he had offered me the job that I might have another baby and so he was not surprised when I told him that I was pregnant.

Rupert was due on Christmas Day. He has always been a person in a hurry and this was evident when he decided to arrive three and a half weeks early. I had been listening to the Budget – it was the first time that it had been delivered in November. I was sitting by the dealing desk on the fund management floor at Morgan Grenfell, surrounded by the other members of the UK team, waiting for something interesting to be announced. Suddenly I was overcome with pain. I thought I was going into labour, but nothing more happened and so I assumed that it must have been a false contraction. That evening, I was writing letters when I had another violent pain. Tim was at a dinner and Joan was at her flat so I was all alone in the house with three children. I lay down on my bed and there were no more pains. I eventually drifted off into a deep sleep. At 2.30 a.m. I awoke with another terrible pain. Then there was another. Then another. I woke Tim and he rang Joan while

I packed some things into a bag. I could not believe that the baby was coming so early.

When he was born an hour later, Rupert had the umbilical cord round his neck. He had suffered a large amount of bruising and he was not breathing properly. The poor little thing was wrapped up, put into a perspex cot and rapidly wheeled over to the Special Care Baby Unit (SCBU) on the other side of the hospital.

Tim went with the nurse and a doctor and, when I had had a couple of stitches, I found myself alone and without my baby. I was desperately worried. A few minutes later, Tim returned with an instamatic photograph of Rupert in SCBU with tubes coming out of every part of his body. Tim asked for a wheelchair and then wheeled me along miles of corridors in the basement of the hospital. We ended up in a different building on the second floor. I could spot Rupert a mile off. He had been very early, but he still weighed 8 lb 5 oz. There were four other babies in there and none of them weighed more than 2 lb.

Rupert was in SCBU for twenty-four hours. The nurses said that it was important to get him to suck as much as possible and they suggested that I could come over to feed him every two hours. I became an expert on the underground passages that lay beneath St Mary's Hospital in Paddington. I was so excited when Rupert was allowed to come back to my room. That was not the end of our stay in the hospital, however. Because he was so early, he had extremely bad jaundice and we were there for another week.

I had two clear weeks before Christmas. As Rupert had been due on Christmas Day, I had been careful to make sure that I had bought and wrapped all the presents well in advance. I had even written all the Christmas cards. I suddenly realized that they had been prepared without Rupert's name on them. They were all sealed and so I could not add his name.

I returned to work at the beginning of April, feeling that there was little difference to my life in having four rather than three children. I found that while I was away from the office, I could look at the business more objectively. It was continuing to go from strength to strength, but I could see that we were getting slightly overstretched in some areas and so I set about doing some recruitment. An excellent candidate came in for an interview when I was still officially on maternity leave. Rupert sat in a corner of the room in his car seat whilst I talked to my potential recruit. Halfway through, the baby woke up and started screaming at the top of his voice. The noise was so bad that I had to take Rupert to another room and console him with a quick feed, leaving the interviewee by himself for twenty minutes. It must have been the most unusual interview that he had ever had. I was concerned that he would decline our offer after this, but luckily I was wrong.

We had won many more new clients during 1993 than I had expected and I had been forced to increase my budget for 1994. We did considerably better than the figure that I had budgeted for. In particular, Keith and I pitched for a number of very large funds and were surprised when we won most of them. I had a huge amount of work on my hands as a result, but it is fun getting to grips with a new portfolio and reorganizing it. The outgoing fund manager had usually been removed because performance was poor and so I needed to change the portfolios to reflect our favoured stocks. The good performance kept rolling in as a result of good teamwork. I was very proud of what Keith and I had created. I was convinced that we had the best team in London. We had put in the really hard work and now we were reaping the rewards.

eight

Tim and I took Georgie, Alice and Serena skiing in Courchevel in April 1995. Rupert was only eighteen months old and there would have been nothing for him to do if he and Joan had come with us, so they stayed at home. Georgie had been off treatment for three and a half years and in remission for five and a half years. She was going to the hospital for a blood test and a check-up every two months and there was no sign of a relapse. As time went on, this was becoming less likely and I was beginning to relax.

When we arrived at the hotel in Courchevel, Georgie complained that she did not feel well. I was not surprised since the rest of us had had a virus before we came. Georgie had the same symptoms, a sore throat and a headache, and so I thought that the bug had finally got her too.

On our third day, Georgie was still feeling unwell. All she wanted to do was sleep and she would not eat a thing. I was beginning to get worried and I asked the hotel to arrange for a doctor to come and see her. He examined her and said that it looked like a virus and that she would probably recover in a day or two. I mentioned that she had had leukaemia and he suggested that I should have a blood test done when we returned to London. Georgie was already booked in to go to Great Ormond Street a couple of days after we arrived back for her normal check-up. The next day, she was a great deal better and by the end of the week she was skiing all day. I was very relieved.

We arrived at Great Ormond Street as usual and went to the haematology laboratory so that Georgie could have a blood test. As it was the school holidays, Alice was with us and I had to tell them off several times for giggling and being silly. On the way to day-care, the girls ran ahead of me, making a beeline for the hospital shop. By the time I got there, they had blocks of paper, stickers and drinks in their hands. I did not have the energy to argue with them. I just bought it all. When we arrived in day-care, Georgie and Alice sat on either side of the play specialist and began to make Easter bunnies. I read a magazine.

I have spent hours sitting in the day-care centre over the years. I know all the staff very well and many of the other families. Occasionally I see a new couple, sitting with a frail child and looking desperately worried. I immediately think of the day when Georgie was first diagnosed and I know exactly what they are going through. We were due to be seen at 11 a.m. and I knew that we would not have to wait for too long.

Georgie was seeing a different doctor to usual that day, but we did know him. He came out and called her. Georgie and Alice groaned as they had not quite finished their creations.

'Come on, you can't keep the doctor waiting. Georgie, come on!'

The doctor told me that the blood test was fine and asked me how Georgie had been. I explained that she had been unwell in France, but that I thought it was the same bug that we had had. He examined her and then said that she could start coming for check-ups every three months instead of two. I was pleased. I felt that another milestone had been reached.

I was still on holiday and so did not have to rush back to work after we left the hospital. Serena and Rupert had gone out with Joan, so I decided to take Georgie and Alice shopping in Harvey Nichols. We had just moved house and there were one or two things that I needed to buy like mugs for the kitchen and a couple of new waste-paper baskets. As at Great Ormond Street, the girls were in high spirits and I was convinced that they were going to break something as I stood in the china department choosing mugs.

'Will you stop being so silly, Georgie. You really are behaving like an idiot today.' Hysterical giggles greeted each reprimand. I scowled at them both. When we had finished on the home furnishing floor, we went up to the restaurant for lunch – Georgie and Alice ate grilled chicken and drank peach nectar.

I had ordered a new bed for Georgie to go in her bedroom in the new house and it had arrived that morning whilst we were out. She had asked for a four-poster bed, but I thought that would be a little over the top and so I had asked a blacksmith in North Wales who had done some work for my parents to make a lit polonaise for her. It had four pieces of metal that went above the bed and met in a central point. Fabric was draped over the metal and tied. It looked like a four-poster bed to her. The curtain maker had made the drapes to go over it and had just put the finishing touches to it when we arrived home. Georgie and Alice went running up the stairs at high speed, desperate to see it. I was about to follow them, but was handed a piece of paper by one of the builders. On it was written, 'Please ring Dr Leiper at Great Ormond Street Hospital urgently.'

My heart sank. There was only one telephone working in the house as the builders were still there and the telephone system was the last thing to be dealt with. What was to be Joan's room was being used as their office. It was half plastered and there were building materials everywhere. There was a trestle-table and an old chair for the foreman to sit at with the telephone on it. I got through to Alison Leiper straight away. Her tone was sombre and my stomach began to churn. I knew that it was bad news. They had had another look at the slide of Georgie's blood and there was something that looked a bit odd. She asked if I could bring her back the next day for another blood test and possibly a bone marrow test.

'Can't I bring her now?'

'No, I think it's better to wait until tomorrow. Can you bring her at 2.30 p.m. I won't be in tomorrow, I'm afraid, but I've arranged for Jane Pasmore to see you.'

'Do you think she's relapsed?' I asked.

'I hate having to discuss these things over the phone,' Alison replied. 'It doesn't look good, though. It could be the virus that you said she had on holiday. Sometimes viruses can distort things, so you must not assume that she has definitely relapsed. We'll have a good look tomorrow.'

I knew she had relapsed. I sat on the plastic chair with my head in my hands, fighting back tears. How could life be so unfair? Georgie had been so well. I thought she was cured. I had spent most of the day telling her off because she was so full of energy. How could she have relapsed? I rang Tim and told him the news. He promised to come home early and to go to the hospital with Georgie and me the next day. My heart was pounding and I felt sick. There was no point in telling anyone else just in case it was a false alarm.

I walked very, very slowly from the basement to the third floor where Georgie and Alice were happily bouncing on Georgie's new bed.

'It's lovely. I adore it. Thank you, thank you, Mummy.' Georgie pulled me on to the bed with her. I put my arms round her and hugged her very tight.

'What's the matter, Mummy? You look so sad,' Alice said.

'I've just spoken to Alison Leiper on the phone, Georgie, and we have to go back to Great Ormond Street tomorrow.'

'Why?'

'Because they looked at your blood again and they thought that they saw something funny.'

'Do they think that the leukaemia has come back again?'

I paused. 'They think it might have, but they can't be sure. That's why they want us to go back.'

Georgie began to howl and soon became hysterical. 'NO! NO! NO! I don't want it to come back, Mummy. I don't want it to come back.' Tears rolled down my face and then Alice began to cry too. We all lay in a wet and tangled heap on the new bed, each trying to comfort the others.

I realized that dealing with an eight-year-old with leukaemia was going to be difficult. Georgie was old enough to understand that she might die and I knew that she would take the loss of her hair badly. When she was two, she had hardly been aware of what was happening to her. After a while, she had thought it perfectly normal to go to the hospital and have anaesthetics. At eight, Georgie knew that this was not normal. There were no other seriously ill children at her school.

Tim, Georgie and I went to the hospital the next day. We barely spoke in the car on the way there. We went back to the lab for another blood test, then to day-care to await the result. Ten minutes after we had arrived, a doctor came and told us that the blood result had already come through. Usually we had to wait for at least an hour for blood results. We were told that it still looked odd and so they were going to do the bone marrow test. Georgie started to cry, not because she was frightened about the outcome of the test, but because she did not want a needle to be stuck in her to administer the anaesthetic. Some cream was put on her hand to numb it, despite her protestation that it never worked. Eventually, she was persuaded that to have a bone marrow test without an anaesthetic would be considerably more painful than the needle. I left the room where the procedure was to be performed and sat with Tim in a four-bed ward waiting for the nurse to tell me that Georgie was ready.

Georgie slept for a long time after the anaesthetic as she always does. Half an hour after the marrow had been taken, we were summoned into one of the consulting rooms to see Jane Pasmore. We both sat down and waited to be told what we thought we already knew.

'I'm afraid that Georgie has relapsed.' There was silence for a few seconds whilst Jane waited for us to take in what she had said. 'Whilst it is not good news, there are several points in Georgie's favour. We have caught the relapse very early which is obviously good, but the most important thing is that she has been in remission for so long. Also, relative to what we give children who are newly diagnosed today, she did not have much chemo the first time round, which means that we can throw everything at it this time. The protocol that we are going to use is called R1 and it is a hard-hitting treatment which is achieving good results. We will be putting a Hickman line in and starting treatment next week. Is there anything you want to ask?' Just as when we were first told that Georgie had leukaemia, I knew there were hundreds of things I should ask, but I could not think of them. Even though we had convinced ourselves that Georgie had relapsed and thought we were prepared to be told this, Tim and I were in a state of shock.

We went back to Georgie's bed. She was still asleep. I had managed not to cry until that point, but when I saw my little girl lying peacefully in the hospital bed, I could control myself no longer. There were some other people in the room and I felt embarrassed, so I went out into the corridor and stood in a corner trying to hide my tears. The sister came up to me and put her arm around me.

'It's better to let it out rather than bottle it up. Everyone understands how you feel. Do you need some more tissues?' I had an enormous lump in my throat and could barely speak. I nodded and she got me a box.

As Georgie began to wake up, she looked into my tear-stained face and she knew that confirmation of her relapse had come. Tears began to pour down her face.

'I don't want to have leukaemia again. I don't want it, Mummy.' I began to cry again. Somehow, it was much worse than the first time. I had thought that if Georgie ever relapsed, I would recognize the signs. I had been worried when she had had the virus in France, but she had got better. The fact that there had been no warning made it very difficult for me to come to terms with the relapse.

That evening, I sat in the builders' office in the basement of our new house and telephoned everyone whom I thought should know about Georgie's relapse. First I spoke to my parents who took it remarkably calmly. I could not get hold of Tim's father and so left a message on his answerphone. Next I rang Keith Percy, my boss. He was very sympathetic and said that I should take as much time off as I needed. I had managed to hold back the tears during these conversations, but when I spoke to Georgie's godfather, Andrew Arends, I started to cry and just could not stop. He was very understanding and gently told me that I had to pull myself together for Georgie's sake. That was the last telephone call I made that evening.

Although the doctors felt that the R1 protocol was the best course of treatment for Georgie, they thought that it would be sensible to test the other children to see if we had a bone marrow match. If Georgie relapsed again, either during R1 or afterwards, this would be the only way left to save her. Tim and I knew that although there was a one in four chance that each child would match, this did not mean that we would have one. It is like throwing a dice and trying to get a six. Sometimes it takes more than six goes to get one. We explained to the children that they were going to have their blood taken and that they might be able to help Georgie. They were all very brave and I was extremely proud of them. Not one of them cried and as they were only aged six, four and one, I thought this was amazing.

A few days later, we were told that none of our three children was a match for Georgie. Although I knew that the doctors would still have gone for R1 even if one of them had been a match, I was very upset. What would happen if Georgie relapsed again? I asked if it would be possible to look for an unrelated donor and was told that the hospital would only do this if she did relapse again. I needed the comfort of knowing that if she did relapse again, she would definitely still have a chance of survival. I needed to know that she had a donor. Life was tough with four children and a responsible job, but I began to think about the possibility of having a fifth child.

I soon discovered that a great deal had changed since Georgie first got leukaemia. Where as we had had to stay in hospital for nine weeks the first time, I was told that this time the treatment would largely be given in day-care and that, if I wished, I could have training so that I could take blood and give drugs intravenously at home. Only if Georgie's temperature went up when her blood counts were very low would we have to stay in hospital and even then, if her temperature stayed down for forty-eight hours, I would be allowed to finish giving the antibiotics at home. If Georgie felt like it, she could even go to school.

Being in hospital for long periods was difficult when I only had one other child and it would have been even more difficult with three so I was relieved when I was told this. Georgie was absolutely delighted. She is very clever and loves school.

'But, Mummy, my hair's going to fall out. I can't go to school with no hair!'

'Don't worry, darling, we'll get you a wig.'

When Georgie was two and she lost her hair, she was delighted. We used to have awful fights about hair washing and not having any meant that this was not an issue. Georgie has beautiful, strawberry-blonde hair and everyone always comments on it. Now it had grown quite long and she loved having French plaits and other complicated hairstyles. The prospect of it all falling out was devastating and was the thing that concerned her most.

Six days after we had been told of her relapse, Georgie and I went into Great Ormond Street overnight for the Hickman line to be put in and the first dose of chemotherapy to be administered. The drug that was being given was called epirubicin and it was similar to the drug that had been used to get Georgie into remission the first time she had leukaemia. It had to be given over a number of hours.

I was told that it was normal for children to get some sort of infection within a few days of having the drug as it completely suppressed the immune system.

For the first few days after Georgie had had the epirubi-cin, she seemed really well. She went to school each day and I went to work. At first my colleagues were surprised to see me, but I explained that the current treatment was designed to enable daily life to continue as normally as possible. I went to client meetings, managed my funds and generally got on with things. You never get over the shock of being told that your child has leukaemia or has relapsed, but you learn to live with it. I found that I could temporarily escape from the anxiety and the worry by concentrating on my work and there was never any shortage of things to do when I was in the office.

Two weeks after Georgie was given the drug, she was still well. We had not been to our house in Hampshire for a couple of weeks because I was worried that Georgie might get an infection when we were there and then we would have to go to the hospital in Winchester where they did not know her. That weekend, we decided to risk it. It was the beginning of May and the weather was perfect. There were tulips out everywhere and the copper beeches had regained their leaves after the winter. The house was a wreck when we bought it and had been left empty for seven years, so we were staying in a small cottage in the grounds while the builders renovated the main house. Rapid progress was being made and, the minute that we arrived, Tim was climbing up the scaffolding looking at what the builders had done since we were last there.

The next evening, we were invited to dinner with friends in the next village. I was a little worried about leaving Georgie, but we had had the same lady looking after the house and doing the baby-sitting for years and she knew the children very well. I gave her the telephone number of our friends and asked her to check Georgie regularly to make sure that she was not hot. As we ate dinner, I listened for the telephone. It would not have surprised me if Georgie's temperature had gone up just at that moment and I had had to leave the dinner party. But there was no telephone call.

When we returned, I went into Georgie's room and felt her head. She had her duvet wrapped round her tightly and was warm, but I was sure that that was because of the bedding. I uncovered her a little and then went to have my bath. When I had finished, I felt her again and was certain that her temperature was normal.

The next morning, Georgie awoke with a high temperature and I immediately rang the hospital in Winchester. They agreed to admit her and we all piled into the car. We only had one car down there and so Tim and the children had to come too. I had a sheet from Great Ormond Street explaining what needed to be done. The paediatric senior registrar examined her thoroughly and then the nurses did some blood cultures and administered the first dose of antibiotics. Georgie looked very pale, but seemed to be in reasonably good spirits. I had been waiting for so long for her to get an infection that I was not surprised. I was sure that the antibiotics would deal with it and that we would be allowed home within a couple of days.

Later that day, Georgie complained that her bottom was hurting. She said that it had been sore for a couple of days. I had a look and I could see a little anal tear. I knew that one of the drugs she was on caused constipation and so I told her that she would have to eat plenty of fruit and drink lots of fluids. She continued to complain and so when the doctor came to see her the next day, I asked her about it. By this stage, it was looking very sore indeed. We were due to go back to London as the other children had to go to school and we were to be transferred to our local hospital there. Great Ormond Street cannot cope with every child with an infection because it needs its beds for the difficult cases and the more complicated parts of the treatment. The doctor told me to ask for a surgeon to look at Georgie's bottom when we got to the local hospital.

I was a little nervous about taking Georgie in the car back to London in such a delicate state, but the hospital seemed to think that it would be all right. There was not much that an ambulance crew could have done that we could not and the journey would probably have taken longer. Tim and I made Georgie comfortable in the car and she soon fell asleep, weakened by the infection and the fact that she had eaten little over the previous two days. When we arrived in London, we stopped at home momentarily to get Georgie some clean pyjamas and some books and tapes before going on to the local hospital.

The nurses were expecting us and welcomed Georgie. It was the first time that she had been an in-patient there. We were given a cubicle with its own bathroom as Georgie needed to be isolated from the other patients because of her lack of immunity. A doctor came to examine her.

'How are you feeling, Georgie?' she asked.

'My bottom hurts.'

'Shall we have a look. Oh, yes, it does look sore doesn't it. When did you last have some paracetamol? I'll ask the nurse to bring you some more.'

As she made for the door, I intervened.

'The doctor in Winchester said that Georgie needed to be seen by a surgeon as soon as possible.'

'The consultant who is responsible for her will be round in the morning and you should ask him about that.'

'She's in terrible pain. Paracetamol doesn't seem to do much for her. She's in absolute agony when she goes to the loo. I don't think it can wait,' I said, beginning to feel exasperated.

'She's on very strong intravenous antibiotics,' the doctor replied, 'and I'm sure that they will deal with the problem, but we'll ask the consultant about it tomorrow. In the meantime, I'll prescribe a stronger painkiller.' She left the room.

Georgie spent a very uncomfortable night. I was lying next to her on a makeshift bed. She tossed and turned and muttered about her bottom hurting and occasionally whimpered. I was ready to give the consultant a piece of my mind if he did not do something about it in the morning. When he came to see Georgie the next morning, he took the same line as the doctor who had seen her the night before. I questioned him hard, but he assured me that the antibiotics would do the trick. There was nothing more to be done.

'Have you spoken to Great Ormond Street about her?' I asked.

'Yes, we have been in regular contact with them and they agree that the treatment we are giving is appropriate.'

'In Winchester, they said she needed to see a surgeon.'

'Well, I've had a good look and I don't think that is necessary. It is sore, but it all looks clean and in a few days it will heal up.' It is very difficult to argue with someone who has superior knowledge. The fact that Georgie had not eaten for several days, was almost delirious because of the severity of the pain and looked terrible told me that there was something pretty wrong. I did not want to ring up Great Ormond Street myself, because I knew that Georgie would have to come to the local hospital regularly and I did not want to destroy our relationship with them on our first visit.

On Wednesday, the third day in the local hospital, Georgie was even worse. At times she was barely conscious, the pain was so bad. I picked up my mobile phone (the use of which was still allowed at that stage), rang one of the symptom care team at Great Ormond Street and asked for her help. She was someone whom I particularly trusted as she used to be the sister on the ward.

'It is very difficult for me to come and see you when you are in another hospital,' she said. 'I don't want to look as though I'm checking up on them.' There was a pause as she thought how the situation could best be handled. 'Well,

I suppose there's nothing wrong with me dropping in to see how Georgie is. It's perfectly reasonable for me to do that as part of her pastoral care.'

'If you don't mind coming, it would make me feel a lot better.'

She looked very concerned when she saw Georgie. She asked me which antibiotics had been given. Like everyone else, she felt that I should give the antibiotics a little longer to work, but if I was still worried in a couple of days, I should ring one of the doctors at Great Ormond Street.

Georgie seemed to be a little better on the Thursday and ate a little; I thought that the antibiotics were finally beginning to take effect. The consultant did not come to see her, but I was assured that he would be in the next day. The following day, I was due to go to Great Ormond Street for intravenous training and I had arranged for my father to sit with Georgie. When I arrived at GOS, various nurses came up and asked how Georgie was. One of them said that I should contact her if Georgie's bottom was still bad when I got back to the local hospital and she would get one of the doctors to ring me.

When I got back, my father was in a terrible state. The consultant had come to look at her and had rushed out of the door in a panic. A procession of doctors had then been in to look at her. Some were dermatologists, others were surgeons. All had appeared to be extremely concerned about her condition. I went out into the main ward, but there were no doctors there who could tell me what was going on. I was in a state of high anxiety. Georgie was lying on her bed looking almost lifeless. When I spoke to her, she barely registered.

It did not matter what the local hospital thought, the most important thing was to get Georgie to Great Ormond Street as quickly as possible. I rang day-care and asked to speak to one of Georgie's consultants, Dr Alison Leiper.

'She's with a patient at the moment. Can I get her to ring you back?' said the nurse.

'I need to speak to her urgently. Is it possible to interrupt?'

'Just a moment.' I was put through to Alison and explained what had happened.

'I'm going to arrange for an ambulance to bring her here so that we can see what's going on. Keep calm. You stay with Georgie and I'll arrange everything.' At that moment, the consultant walked in.

'I am talking to Alison Leiper and she wants Georgie to go to Great Ormond Street immediately,' I said.

'I was about to ring her to suggest the same thing,' he replied rather sheepishly.

The next twenty-four hours were the worst of my entire life. It seemed to take an age for the ambulance to arrive. I had my car in the car park and I asked why I could not take her myself. The nurses said that she was too sick and there was no choice but to go in an ambulance. Eventually, the ambulance arrived, but the crew refused to come up to the ward to collect Georgie. I could not believe it. One of the nurses and I started to wheel her down and the others gathered round to wish Georgie well. I knew they meant it, but I could not help feeling angry with them for allowing her to get into such a terrible state. I did not really understand what was wrong with Georgie, but I was beginning to suspect that her life was in danger.

When we arrived at Great Ormond Street, Georgie was taken to her usual ward. It was an enormous relief to be in familiar surroundings. I had telephoned Tim at the office just before we had left and he was waiting for us when we arrived.

'She looks terrible,' he said as the ambulance crew wheeled her in. They had at least agreed to take her from the ambulance to the ward. 'What do you think is wrong with her?'

'I don't know, but it doesn't look too good.'

My concerns were reinforced when Alison Leiper arrived. Over the many years that Georgie and I had been going to Great Ormond Street, Alison and I had become friends. She went white when she saw Georgie and I could tell from her expression that Georgie's condition was very serious. Tim and I questioned her anxiously, but she was pretty non-committal, saying only that she would arrange for the infectious diseases doctor and the surgeon to come and look at her as soon as possible. I began to shake with fear. What was wrong with Georgie? What would the surgeon be able to do? I had figured out in my own mind that it would be sensible to do a colostomy, but would that be all that was needed?

A friend of ours rang to find out how Georgie was. I was amazed that she had managed to locate us. She had rung the local hospital and been told that we had transferred to Great Ormond Street and somehow she had found the right ward. Many years before she had been a nurse at the hospital and she had always been a tower of strength throughout Georgie's illness. When I told her what was happening, she and her husband jumped into the car and came over to see us. This was a particularly kind gesture as they had four children who they had to get someone to look after, they lived miles away and it was a Friday night.

The infectious diseases doctor, Dr Novelli, said that he would change the antibiotics and see if that had any effect, but that we should wait to see what the surgeon thought.

The surgeons' senior registrar came in first, took one look at Georgie and said that he would get Mr Kiely, one of the most respected and best children's surgeons in the country, to come immediately. Just before our friends arrived, Mr Kiely came in to see Georgie. As he examined her, he looked pensive. Tim and I waited patiently for him to give his view, but he seemed deep in thought. I could not bear the suspense any longer.

'Does she need to have a colostomy?' I asked.

'That is the first thing that we have to do and we need to do that now. When did she last eat or drink?' Unfortunately, she had been given something to drink when we had arrived two hours before and so that meant that she could not be given an anaesthetic for another two hours. Mr Kiely spoke slowly and deliberately, looking at the floor instead of at Tim and me. 'The decision we have to make is whether to cut away the infected flesh at the same time. I understand that the antibiotics are being changed. I am doubtful that they will stop the progression of the infection, but what I will do is ask the nurse to draw around the red areas on her buttocks with a Biro so that we can see how much worse or better it has got by the morning. We will then decide tomorrow whether we have to cut away any flesh. That will mean that she may need two general anaesthetics, but I am afraid that the colostomy is urgent as we need to keep the infected area as clean as possible.'

I could see that it was necessary to stop the faeces coming down as normal. What had started as a small anal tear had become a blackened, angry-looking wound and both of Georgie's buttocks were now bright red. We were told that the colostomy would be a temporary one. An incision would be made on the left-hand side of her tummy and then a hole would be made in the colon. They would then pull the colon out and stitch it to her skin. A sticky round thing would then be stuck over it and a bag attached to catch the faeces. All that was happening in effect was that the faeces were being diverted in order to allow the doctors to deal with the problem.

Our friends, Peter and Sheila, arrived and I told them what Mr Kiely had said and that Georgie would be going down to the operating theatre in a couple of hours. Sheila put her arms around me and told me not to worry. She said that they would stay until Georgie came out of theatre. I went down with Georgie as usual and got the same sinking feeling as she lost consciousness that I always get. I will never get over the fear of never seeing her again when she has an anaesthetic. I had kept very calm all day, but as I walked back from the theatre with the nurse, I was fighting back tears.

It always seems as though time is passing very slowly when you are waiting for your child to come out of theatre.

Tim, Peter, Sheila and I sat trying to have a normal conversation. Every now and then, Sheila would say, 'Don't worry. She'll be all right. You're in the best place and Mr Kiely is an excellent surgeon.'

Before Georgie returned, we were taken to a different ward where the nursing was more intensive and the standards of hygiene were even more rigorously controlled. People coming in and out of the room were required to wash their hands with special disinfectant soap and put on plastic aprons. No one who had had any recent infections was allowed in. When Georgie came back, she was on a morphine drip and was completely out of it. Peter and Sheila had to return home to relieve their baby-sitter. It had been a great comfort having someone there to help us through a difficult evening. Georgie seemed stable. The big question was how much worse the red area on her bottom would be the next morning.

Tim and I both stayed at the hospital that night and Joan stayed at home with the other children. There was not enough room for both of us to sleep with Georgie and so the nurses gave Tim a bed in an empty room. I barely slept, wondering if the infection was getting better or worse. Every now and then, Georgie would emit a groan and I would leap up and hold her hand.

'It's all right, darling. Mummy's here.' She would mumble something incomprehensible and then drift back into a restless sleep. There were drip stands everywhere with bags of fluid in them and she had a catheter. Her hair had fallen out as a result of the chemotherapy and she had lost ten kilos in weight. She was unrecognizable as the child who had been running around Harvey Nichols three weeks before.

The next morning, Mr Kiely arrived early. I had not dared look at Georgie's bottom to see if the red area had spread beyond the Biro marks. The nurse rolled her on to her side. She was still wearing the operating gown from the night before. Not only had the red area increased, but there was a purple area in the middle of her right buttock. Mr Kiely was in no doubt. She had to be operated on as soon as possible.

Everyone swung into action. Doctors came in and out. Tears started rolling down my face when I was alone for a moment with Georgie. Tim was still asleep and I did not want to wake him. I thought Georgie was asleep too, but she suddenly opened her eyes. I did not want her to see me crying and so I disappeared into the bathroom for a moment and splashed cold water on my face to try and disguise it. I sat by the bed and held her hand.

'You've been crying, Mummy. Why?'

'I haven't been crying, darling, I've just got a bit of a cold.' I smiled at her and kissed her hand, but I could see that she did not believe me.

One of the haematologists came in to see Georgie and explained that she still did not have any neutrophils, the white cells in the blood that fight bacterial infection, but there was a drug that she could give that might boost them. They would also try and find a donor to give white cells and do a transfusion. They had not done a white cell transfusion for years as there was some doubt as to whether it made any difference and it could be dangerous, but

Georgie's case was so serious that they had to throw everything at the infection to stop it.

Tim had woken up and he looked at me uneasily when I showed him Georgie's bottom. We sat and waited for the operating trolley to come in silence. My heart was pounding and I felt sick. Only one of us was allowed to go down with her, even in such a serious situation, and so I went, leaving poor Tim alone in the room. Georgie was carefully lifted on to the trolley. She was sore as a result of the colostomy and was vociferous in her objection to being moved. The morphine had made her aggressive and she was very rude to the nurses who were trying to be as gentle as possible. She clasped my hand as we walked along the corridors on the same journey as the previous evening and she would not let go. I was not sure how much she had absorbed of what was going on and I did not want to frighten her by telling her.

We reached the ante-room to the operating theatre and the anaesthetist came in. She asked all the usual questions about allergies, breathing problems, etc. Somehow we got into conversation and she told me that she had been trained at Guy's Hospital. I discovered that she knew one of Georgie's godfathers, Nick Maynard, who had also been there. By this time, Georgie was under. The anaesthetist touched my arm as I was about to go and said with real feeling that she hoped it would work out for us. As I left the room, a flood of tears poured down my face. If there was ever a time when I truly might not see Georgie alive again, it was now. I could tell from the way that everyone was behaving that she was close to death.

Mr Kiely had told me that morning that Georgie would probably be returning to intensive care after the operation and we were taken down there for a tour whilst she was in the theatre. We were shown a cubicle which was packed with machinery. The thought of Georgie lying there surrounded by monitors, barely conscious, filled me with horror, but it would be better than never seeing her again. Whilst she was in that cubicle, there would still be hope. I wanted to ask how many children who came into intensive care came out alive, but I could not bring myself to.

'We still don't really know what she has got or what the chances are of her surviving the operation,' Tim said as we sat and waited in Georgie's old room. The paediatric senior registrar was at the nurse's desk and so Tim decided to ask him to come and talk to us. It was only at that point that we discovered that Georgie had necrotizing fasciitis.

'What exactly is it?' I asked.

'It is when a bacteria gets into the flesh and starts attacking it. It spreads very fast and cuts off the blood supply to each area as it goes. If it gets into a limb, the patient generally has to have it amputated. The only way to stop it is to cut it out.' Tim and I were horrified, and for a few moments were both unable to speak. We realized that our daughter had the flesh-eating disease that had so recently been splashed all over the tabloid newspapers.

'What are the chances of Georgie coming out of the operating theatre alive?' I asked.

'There is no point in me giving you statistical odds,' the doctor said. 'It's impossible to tell in these situations which children are going to make it and which are not. If I was to

219

say that there was only a 10 per cent chance of survival, it would not tell you anything. Georgie might be the lucky one who pulls through.'

'Are you saying that there is only a 10 per cent chance of survival?' He paused and then spoke to me in a very quiet voice. 'Nicola, I think you realize that Georgie's life is in real danger. She is very, very sick. I don't know whether she is going to survive. You should prepare yourself for the worst, but there is still some hope.'

Tim and I were distraught. Georgie had relapsed and we had been told that the R1 protocol was fantastic and was achieving very good results. Now her life was threatened, not by the leukaemia itself, but by an infection which was eating away her body. Neither of us could bear the prospect of losing Georgie. We clung to each other, tears pouring down our faces, helpless to do anything to save her. Mr Kiely was the only person who could do that and it might even be beyond his powers to do so. If her heart gave up when she was on the operating table, that would be it.

I could see no way out now. I was convinced that Georgie was going to die. An hour and a half had passed since she had gone down to theatre and there was still no word. I went to the nurses and, dabbing at my red eyes with a sodden tissue, asked if there was any news. One of them rang down and said that there was no word yet.

Work is the last thing that would normally be on my mind in such circumstances, but Keith Percy was going abroad the next day and I was due to do a presentation on the following Monday for a £750 million account. This was much larger than the normal amount we pitched for and represented the total assets of a small insurance company. If we won it, it would be our second-largest account. I rang Keith and explained what was happening. I needed to tell him that Monday might be difficult, but I also wanted to talk to him as a friend. He could not believe it when I told him that there was a strong possibility that Georgie might die.

'Forget the presentation. I'll get someone else to do it.'

'But they will be expecting to see either you or me. We won't win it.'

'Nicola, you've got to stay with Georgie and it really doesn't matter if we don't win it. Pam and I are thinking of you. Let me know later how Georgie is. Is Tim okay?'

'No.'

'I can't imagine what you two are going through.'

I could not believe what we were going through. Georgie was such a joy to me. She was a sweet-natured child and highly intelligent. When she had had cranial irradiation, I had been told that she might suffer academically and yet she had done brilliantly at school and was expected to get into a top London girls' day school when she had finished at her prep school, Glendower. The worst thing about the situation was how Alice would react. She adored Georgie, worshipped the ground that she walked on. How was I going to tell her if Georgie died. Would she ever recover?

Just after I had put the telephone down, Mr Kiely walked into the room. I could tell from his expression that Georgie was alive. There was even a vague hint of a smile.

'She's pulled through!' I closed my eyes and felt relief

flowing through my body. The butterflies in my stomach were gone. Mr Kiely continued. 'We did not have to remove as much flesh as I thought we would have to. The left buttock is intact. We had to cut quite a lot out of the right buttock, but I think we got all of it out. We will have to take her down to theatre tomorrow and have another look and I can't guarantee that we won't have to do something to the left buttock, but I think it will be okay.'

'Will the colostomy be reversible?' I asked. When the original operation had been done, we had been told that it would only be temporary, but that was before Mr Kiely had cut the infected flesh out.

'Luckily, the infection spread down into the buttock and so there is not too much damage to the sphincter. I think it will be possible to reverse the colostomy in time. There's no need for her to go to intensive care. She'll be brought back here in a minute.'

Tim and I were ecstatic. We had been utterly convinced that we would never see Georgie again. When the trolley arrived, we both fell upon her. She hardly knew we were there because she had had so much morphine, but we needed to touch her, to feel the warmth of her body, to make sure that she really was still alive.

nine

Georgie had survived, but she was in a critical condition for several days after the operation. It was clear, however, that the medical staff were becoming more relaxed about the situation and so Tim and I slowly became less tense. The operation had taken place on the Saturday morning and the next day I suddenly remembered that I had forgotten to ring Keith about the presentation I was due to do on Monday morning. I told him that Georgie had survived and I would be able to do it.

'Are you sure that you want to do it after all that you've just been through?'

'I'm certain. It will be good for me to escape from the hospital for a couple of hours.' I had no idea what I was going to say in the presentation and had not even seen the document that I was to talk about, but I did not want to let Keith down. He had been so kind and understanding about Georgie's illness and had always stood in for me when I was unable to attend important meetings. I knew that he simply could not be there on this occasion and I could.

Because Georgie had just had the colostomy formed, she was not allowed to eat or drink anything for several days. There was a fluid drip, but her mouth was really dry and this was made worse by the anaesthetics.

'I'm thirsty, Mummy. I want a drink. I'm thirsty. Please give me a drink.'

'You know I can't, darling.' The nurses gave me some sterile sponges on sticks and some purified water and told me to wet the sponges and put them in her mouth, but this made little difference and after I had tried it a couple of times, she refused them.

'You'll be able to drink very soon, Georgie,' I said feebly.

Georgie was taken down to theatre again on the Sunday and Mr Kiely was very pleased as there was virtually no sign of the infection. The left buttock was beginning to get better and so it was not necessary to cut any flesh away. The haematologists were still concerned about the fact that her neutophil count was zero and so they decided to go ahead with the white cell transfusion. One of the doctors explained to me that Georgie was in a relatively unusual blood group and that they could not find a blood donor to give white cells. Donating involved sitting on a machine for three hours whilst the white cells were spun off and so it would be a real act of kindness if anyone came forward.

I pointed out that I was the same blood group as Georgie and at first the doctor was not keen to use me, but it was not clear why. When a donor still had not been found by lunch-time, it was decided that it would be possible to use me. My blood was cross-matched with Georgie's and an HIV test was done, a standard requirement now when you are giving blood. I was all ready to go to University College Hospital when I was told that a donor had been found. Later that afternoon, Georgie was given the white cells and promptly came out in a bright red rash all over her body. I rushed out to find a doctor and it was decided that it was an allergic reaction. Antihistamine was given and the rash subsided.

Georgie had been given an air bed to ensure that she did not get bed sores and to cushion the extensive wounding that she had as a result of the operation. She was very comfortable on the air bed, but the controls were complex and completely baffling. Once or twice, the bed started to deflate spontaneously and there would be a major panic. I would run out of the room, summon a nurse who would press a few buttons and then nothing would happen. The bed was hired from a specialist medical equipment company and they would be summoned to reflate the bed. Luckily, they were always very prompt in answering our calls for help.

The nurses seemed to think that it would be many weeks before Georgie would even be able to walk, never mind leave the hospital. As she was not moving at all, it was important that she did some leg exercises. She had already spent several days in bed and her legs were beginning to look very thin and wasted. A lovely physiotherapist called Alison came to do the exercises with her every day. At first Georgie was very unco-operative; the effects of the morphine were still noticeable.

I had barely seen my other children over the previous eight days and I was missing them terribly. Rupert was only eighteen months old and the others were still small. We thought that it would be fine for them to visit Georgie for a short period that afternoon. When Alice came into the room, she went running up to Georgie's bed and touched her hand. She had a canular in it for one of the drips and she shrieked in exaggerated pain.

'You silly little girl! How dare you hurt me. Go away.' The morphine was speaking again. This was not my darling Georgie. Alice's little face fell and she took a few steps back. I grabbed her hand and whispered in her ear that Georgie could not help being horrid. It was the medicine that was making her like that. Alice nodded as I talked and was very brave about it. I could see that she felt hurt, but she tried not to show it.

It was chaos in a small room with the air bed and all the controls were at Rupert's level, so Tim took him and Serena to the playroom for a while. Alice stayed with me and Georgie began to warm to her after a few minutes. By the time Tim was ready to go, they were talking to each other as they always did.

'What's happened to Georgie's hair, Mummy?' Alice whispered as she was going.

'I told you it was going to fall out, darling. Don't worry, it'll grow back.'

Georgie had a much more peaceful night and I slept really well too. That was just as well as I was due to do the presentation the next day. Tim had brought me some work clothes and I put them on when I woke up. Georgie was going down to the operating theatre again to have her wound dressed and cleaned. One of the nurses from the ward had asked if she could watch as she wanted to see how extensive the surgery had been. She said I could go too, but that was the last thing that I wanted to do. I am not particularly squeamish, but I was worried about looking at Georgie's bottom. I had no idea how extensive the removal of flesh had been and I was too frightened to look. It had not been grafted yet and I did not know what flesh without skin would look like.

When she came back from the theatre, the nurse told me that the infection had continued to subside and the wound was looking very clean. Mr Kiely's senior registrar came to see me and told me that it would be necessary to take Georgie down to theatre every day for the rest of the week. If the wound was still clean and not infected in any way by Friday, then the whole area would be grafted. Most people worry about having the occasional anaesthetic. Georgie had already had four in four days and by the end of the week she was expected to have had a further four.

I left for the office at the last possible moment and my mother stayed with Georgie. It felt very strange going to work. It was only ten days since I had been to the office, but it seemed as though months had passed. Everyone greeted me in a low-key way and said they were sorry to hear that Georgie had been so ill. I picked up the presentation booklet and went upstairs to the meeting room. I had never met these potential clients before, but they were very friendly. They had no idea that my daughter had nearly died two days before and that she still was not completely out of the woods. For all they knew, I had been in the office all morning.

I had two colleagues with me and luckily it was one of

them who did the introduction. If I had had to do the first part, I would have stumbled over my words, something that I never usually did. Usually when I made presentations, it was just part of a normal day's work. This time I felt out of practice; not nervous, just rusty. My turn soon came. I had to concentrate very hard when I started speaking, but soon I relaxed and after a few minutes I began to feel as though nothing had happened and it was just another day at work. I could sense that there was a real rapport with the people on the other side of the table. They nodded and smiled as I spoke.

When the presentation was over, the prospective client left and one of my colleagues put his arm round me. 'Well done! You were very brave.' It was not really brave. In fact it had made me feel much better to escape from the hospital and return to the outside world if only for a short time. I bade everyone goodbye, jumped into a taxi and returned to the hospital.

Georgie was looking a great deal better. The pain had reduced considerably and so she did not need as much morphine and her mood had improved dramatically as a result. The aggression that had been evident when Alice had come to visit her had gone. She was beginning to get bored. Any movement made her bottom hurt and so she had to lie virtually flat and very still. There was little that I could do to entertain her and so she watched videos, listened to tapes, I read to her and she read to herself. I designed a reading chart for her and went out and bought her a pile of books. Each time she finished one, I wrote down the book, the author and the date that she finished it. As the days went by, she was able to have the adjustable back of the air bed a little higher and we began to play board games: Boggle, Scrabble, Downfall, Monopoly – there were very few games that we did not play. Plenty of people came to visit her, including teachers and friends from her school.

The wound stayed clean and so the plastic surgeons were able to do the skin grafts at the end of the first week. It was only now that I felt brave enough to look at Georgie's bottom. It would be the first time that I had seen it since she had had surgery. When the doctors had done the skin graft, they had stitched the dressing to Georgie's bottom. The plastic surgeon turned her on her side and cut the dressing away. There was a layer of sticky gauze on top of the wound and he carefully peeled it away. It was an unpleasant sight, made worse by the fact that the wound had been liberally covered in iodine to keep it clean. There are photographs of Georgie's bottom at various stages in her medical notes and every now and then, Georgie persuades Alison Leiper to let her look at them. They are horrific, but she seems to have a morbid fascination with them. The skin for the graft had been taken from the back of Georgie's right leg so she now had another dressing to change. Each day, the plastic surgeon would come and change both dressings. At least the colostomy had healed. It was working well and I had learned how to change it without pressing too hard on Georgie's tummy and hurting her. Her blood counts had even come up.

Once it was clear that the skin grafts had taken, the physiotherapist suggested that she should do some more vigorous exercises. Georgie was happy to co-operate and did everything that was asked of her, but it did not seem to stop her legs wasting. She had lost one-third of her body weight and looked frighteningly thin. Georgie had never liked hospital food and we were lucky that there were kitchen facilities opposite our room. As she got better, she began to regain her appetite and I would cook her meals every evening. I was limited by the lack of an oven, but there was a hob and a microwave so I was able to prepare steak, new potatoes and green beans for her or pasta with tomato sauce. Gradually she began to gain a little weight and I gained a lot as I ate all the food too and had no exercise. For six weeks, Georgie stayed in Great Ormond Street. So much for all the treatment being done on an outpatient basis. So much for it barely affecting our lives. I still could not believe that Georgie had fallen prey to such a rare and devastating side-effect. There seemed to be no explanation for why it had happened.

A couple of days after the presentation, someone rang me from work and told me that we had won the account. I could not believe it. I had managed to do a reasonable job, but it had not been my best performance. Keith rang me.

'Well done. That was a marvellous achievement.'

'It wasn't just due to me. There were two other people making the presentation.'

'Yes, but they were not in your position. You were very brave. How is Georgie?'

'She's fine. We'll be in here for another few weeks. I'll come into the office in a couple of days.'

'You don't have to do that. You stay there with Georgie.'

'No, I need to get out occasionally and I can't stand the thought of that pile of paper on my desk getting ever bigger.' During the weeks that Georgie was in hospital, I would regularly go into the office for a couple of hours at a time. Members of my team would also visit me in the hospital and bring me documents to sign and to read. I was doing another presentation with a colleague called Peter Lees. He came to the hospital and I found a small room where we could have our pre-meet. It seemed rather odd sitting there in my leggings and flip-flops talking about how to approach the presentation.

Georgie was sufficiently well after five weeks to go home, but the physiotherapist, Alison, did not want her to leave until she had started walking again. At first Georgie was frightened to try. Alison enlisted the help of the play specialist, Wendy, to help motivate Georgie to walk. Alison procured a wheelchair and took Georgie down to the playroom in it for a couple of days. Georgie had a wonderful time making things with Wendy and playing games. Each day she would wake up and the first thing she would say was, 'Can I go and see Wendy?'

One day, Alison came in with Wendy and said, 'You can only come down to the playroom if you walk some of the way.'

'But I can't,' Georgie protested and started to cry.

'Yes you can,' said Wendy, 'we'll help you.' Alison took one arm and Wendy took the other and they gently lifted my emaciated daughter out of her bed.

'You're hurting me, you're hurting me,' Georgie whimpered as they attempted to get her to stand. 'Help me,

Mummy. They're hurting me.' We all encouraged her and coaxed her and, finally, she took two well-supported steps. It was as thrilling as seeing a baby walk for the first time. There was a long way to go yet, but I knew that Georgie was really on the road to recovery.

Each day, Georgie walked a little bit further. She got tired very easily and it was necessary to use the wheelchair if she wanted to travel any real distance. By the end of the sixth week, everyone felt that Georgie was mobile enough to go home. Her room was packed and it took Tim and I several journeys down to the car to empty it. Finally we wheeled Georgie down to the car and then remembered that we somehow had to fit the wheelchair in too. Tim lifted Georgie in and then undertook a major reorganization of the boot. In a strange sort of way, I felt sad about leaving the hospital. Georgie and I had been cocooned in there for so many weeks that we had become institutionalized. It seemed odd to be returning to the outside world.

*

Alice, Serena and Rupert were delighted to see Georgie when she arrived home. She managed to take a few steps and then I helped her to sit down on the sofa in the playroom. Rupert was still very small and could not really understand what was going on, but he was very sweet and patted Georgie on the leg. She stroked his little head and smiled at him. She had missed her sisters and brother. The hospital had said that it would be fine for Georgie to go to school if they were happy to have her in that condition. There were only two weeks of the summer term left and

Georgie was very anxious to be there. I rang the headmistress and explained what Georgie's condition was and, to my surprise, she agreed to have her at school for half a day to see how she got on.

Georgie was determined not to go to school with no hair and so I took her to a wig shop. The NHS had several standard wigs to choose from, dark or blonde, short straight, long straight, short curly and long curly. As Georgie's hair is strawberry-blonde, I suggested that we should have a blonde short wig. Georgie preferred the dark one. In the end, the lady said that she would ring Great Ormond Street and ask for permission to let us have both. Permission was granted and Georgie went home, delighted with her new hair.

Georgie wore the blonde wig on her first day back in school. I carried her up three flights of stairs to her classroom. The other girls were delighted to see her, although they found it difficult to recognize her at first and the headmistress asked who the new girl was in assembly. After a couple of days, Georgie could sense that her friends preferred her without the wig and so she abandoned it. I had asked if the shop wanted them back when Georgie had finished with them, but I had been told that they were hers to keep, so they were consigned to the dressing-up basket. Georgie and Alice put one on Rupert one day and took a picture of him. He would have made a very pretty girl!

Georgie survived her first half-day at school very well and it was noticeable that her walking had improved when she returned home. Within a few days, she was running up and down the stairs at school. Her legs were still very wasted, but they were getting stronger each day and she was eating well and putting on a little more of her lost weight.

Tim and I had often talked about whether I should give up work over the course of this crisis and I decided to take his advice and see how things panned out rather than make a rash move that I might subsequently regret. I was prepared to stop at any moment and watched carefully to see whether Georgie was suffering in any way as a result of me continuing to work. At the height of the crisis, I said to Georgie, 'I think it would be a good idea if I gave up work and we moved to the country.'

'No, I don't want to do that,' she insisted. 'I want to stay in London. All my friends are in London and I like my school. Anyway, you would be bored if you didn't work.'

'I could do some work from home. I could write newspaper articles or a book.'

'It wouldn't be the same. You would be bored. I know you would.'

Within a couple of weeks of Georgie coming out of Great Ormond Street, we had moved back into our normal routine. I would leave for work at 7.15 a.m. and return at 6.30 p.m., read each child a story and put them to bed. Georgie resumed her leukaemia treatment and we had to spend three more weeks in hospital over the course of the summer. The weather was very hot and the air-conditioned ward was the best place to be. All the medical staff were amazed when Georgie arrived, walking perfectly and looking plumper only three weeks after she had been allowed to return home.

In September, Georgie was due to have another dose of

epirubicin. I was absolutely convinced that there was a connection between the drug and the necrotizing fasciitis. I discussed the matter with Professor Judith Chessells and we agreed that, to be on the safe side, Georgie would only have two-thirds of the full dose. Judith did not think that this would make a significant difference to Georgie's chances of survival. As I watched the bright red fluid dripping into her, I felt very anxious. Georgie needed this drug to help cure her, but I suspected that it had caused the problems that had nearly cost her her life.

A few days after Georgie had had the epirubicin, she woke up screaming.

'My bottom hurts. Mummy, Mummy, my bottom hurts.' It was pouring with rain outside and I tried to ring Great Ormond Street, but there was no reply from day-care. I kept trying and eventually I got through. Georgie did not want to eat anything, she just wanted to go to the hospital to find out why her bottom was hurting.

I put her in the car and drove up through Notting Hill Gate from our house in Kensington and on to the Bayswater Road. It was still pouring with rain and the traffic was diabolical. Georgie was screaming and it was desperately frustrating to be sitting in a jam with no way out. When I got to the hospital, there was nowhere to park near the main entrance and it was clear that Georgie would not be able to walk any distance. I parked on a yellow line, put the hazard lights on and carried her in through the main entrance.

'Would you mind looking after Georgie whilst I park the car?' I asked one of the volunteers in the main hall. She looked horrified and said that she was not allowed to accept responsibility for children, especially not ones that were screaming with pain.

'Please help me. My car is on a yellow line and it will get towed away.' She agreed and I pelted out of the door, jumped into the car, drove to the car park and then ran as fast as I could back to the hospital. Georgie was calmer, but was clearly in a great deal of pain. The volunteer had procured a wheelchair for her and I pushed her up to daycare. We were put in a cubicle. I could not do anything. I had bought a magazine, but I was too worried to read it. I stroked Georgie's head.

'Does it still hurt?' She grimaced and nodded. Within the hour, Mr Kiely had been to see her, taken her down to the operating theatre and sorted out the problem. I stood outside the theatre waiting for a nurse to wheel Georgie out and Mr Kiely came to speak to me. He looked completely baffled. He had found more necrotizing fasciitis. It was a relatively small area that had been affected, but it was sufficiently large to require another two weeks in hospital and more skin grafting. Necrotizing fasciitis is extremely rare. For Georgie to have had it twice was quite extraordinary, but Mr Kiely's rapid action had limited the damage this time.

As we did not have a bone marrow match, I had decided that I wanted to have another baby. I knew that having five children would be very hard work, but I felt that I would never be able to forgive myself if Georgie relapsed again and no unrelated donors could be found. I was feeling extremely unwell one day as I was sitting in Georgie's room in the hospital and it suddenly occurred to me that my period was a couple of days late. It was possible that I might be pregnant. I went to a small chemist round the corner from the hospital and purchased a home pregnancy test kit. It was easy to use and when I did it, the result was positive. I rushed out of our bathroom and showed it to Georgie.

'Don't be silly, Mummy,' she said, 'you can't be pregnant. You never see Daddy. You're always here with me.' Somehow, between all the hospital visits, I had managed to be at home on the right day.

Tim came to see Georgie at lunch-time that day and we broke the news to him. He sat on my bed with his head in his hands and groaned.

'We can't cope with any more children. Four is a huge number. How are we going to cope with five?'

'Don't say that, Daddy. Mummy and I want another baby.' That put him in his place.

Again Georgie and I attempted to return to some sort of normality. After the second episode of necrotizing fasciitis, she remained well and did not get admitted to hospital again for over a year. The main part of the treatment was over and she went into maintenance. In the R1 protocol, this involves eight twelve-week blocks. For the first six weeks, the patient takes oral medication; then in weeks seven and eight they have a block of chemotherapy. The remainder of the time is spent taking nothing at all while the counts come back up and then the process starts all over again. Georgie was able to tolerate the drugs in the maintenance part of the protocol extremely well.

I had told Georgie that her hair probably would not grow back for four or five months after the second lot of epirubicin, but it started to grow after less than three. I was surprised and she was over the moon. The quality of the hair was not as it had been as the drugs that Georgie was still on affected it, but at least she had some hair and it did make her feel much less self-conscious.

Morgan Grenfell had survived my long absences extremely well and I was pleased that the team that I had built had performed so strongly. It was four years since I had joined the firm and the changes that I had made at the beginning had worked. The track record was getting better and better and the result was that we were winning ever increasing amounts of new business. Keith Percy and I would do the large pitches and as we went into 1996 there were very few that we had not won over the course of the previous year. I had recruited a number of new people and they had settled in and integrated into the team without any problems.

I broke the news of my pregnancy to Keith shortly after Georgie's second bout of necrotizing fasciitis. I explained about the fact that none of my children was a bone marrow match and that I wanted to have one last attempt at producing one. He understood and, although my absence put further pressure on him, he did not mind. I promised that I would work right up to the end of my pregnancy. The baby was due in early June.

Tim had decided to change jobs and ended up being at home for the summer of 1996. I was delighted that we were both going to be at home at the same time. It was the first time that we had been able to spend any length of time together since we had been at university. The baby was one week late and Tim kept trying to persuade me to stop working and keep him company, but I wanted to go into the office until the bitter end. I did not go to any client meetings or company meetings in the last week, but instead made sure that I had dealt with everything on my desk and that all my colleagues were clear as to who was responsible for which aspect of my job.

There was a new technique akin to a bone marrow transplant for children with leukaemia using the blood from a sibling's umbilical cord. I was told by the Cord Blood Bank that I needed to ring them the minute I went into labour and they would come and collect the blood from the cord. I woke up at four o'clock in the morning, realized that the baby was coming, and rang the Cord Blood Bank before the hospital. Tim and I quickly dressed and got in the car. Forty minutes after I had had the first contraction, Antonia was born. The Cord Blood Bank nurses had not arrived, but luckily John Smith, my obstetrician, had taken the precaution of getting one of their kits just in case. He extracted the blood from the umbilical cord himself and had just finished when the nurses arrived.

If Antonia had been a match for Georgie, this could have been a possible route if she relapsed again. In fact, Antonia was not a match for Georgie. Their bone marrow could not have been more different. Why were we always so unlucky? I had a really beautiful baby, though, and it did not matter

that she was not a match for Georgie. I loved her passion-
ately and having her to cuddle made me feel a hundred
times better.

Tim was determined that we were going to make the
most of our time off together and he had encouraged me
to book a holiday in Rome for the middle of June. As the
baby was late, we ended up going when she was only one
week old. Tim had read about a hotel twenty miles north
of Rome which had belonged to John Paul Getty who had
totally refurbished the house and then got bored of it and
sold it. It was right on the edge of the sea. There was no
beach; the water literally came up to the walls of the villa.
Underneath were the remains of Caesar's palace and the
cellars had been converted into a museum with many of
the original mosaics perfectly preserved. The hotel had a
feeling of being in someone's house and it was very relaxing
to sit in bed and listen to the waves lapping against the sea
wall.

I was lucky that I felt so well so soon after the baby's
birth and we spent two days walking around Rome looking
at all the sights. The last time that I had been there was at
the end of my first year at Oxford and I had forgotten how
spectacular it was. I had Antonia in a sling and she slept for
hours as we wandered around. The weather was beautiful
and we returned to London after six days feeling really
refreshed.

I had booked a villa in the South of France for two weeks
in August. We had not had any family holidays abroad since
Georgie's illness and now that she was so well, I thought
that we all deserved some time away as a family. For

months, Keith Percy and I had been talking to a major British company about managing its pension fund and they decided to invite us to make a formal presentation when I was due to be in France. As I had had such close contact with them for so long, I felt that I should fly back to do the presentation with Keith. As I was breast feeding the baby, she would have to come too and my secretary agreed to look after her whilst we were at the company's offices, which were fortunately on the edge of the City.

Antonia and I flew back from Nice and were met by a car at the airport which took us to my office. I handed Antonia over with some trepidation. I had not been parted from her for more than five minutes since she was born. My secretary, Carole, loved babies and was delighted to look after her. As the baby loved her sling so much, I strapped her to Carole and left the building praying that she would behave. The presentation seemed to go well and I rushed out of the building. Carole had brought Antonia back to me in a taxi and she was screaming and screaming. The poor baby had got herself into a terrible state. Sir John Craven was away that week and so I had been lent his chauffeur to take me back to the airport. I think that he was more than a little embarrassed when I started to feed Antonia in the car. It was the only way to stop her howling.

The house that we had rented in France was high up in the hills above Cannes. The views were spectacular and, as there was a pool, we did not need to leave the garden as the children just wanted to swim all day. We did go for the occasional drive and my father-in-law, who came to stay with us for one week, and I took the children to one of the perfume houses in Grasse to learn about how perfume was made. They were fascinated and I bought them all a small bottle of perfume to take home. Rupert got a bar of soap shaped like a duck.

When we returned from France there was still a couple of weeks left before Tim was due to start his new job and I had several more weeks of maternity leave left, so we decided to spend a few weeks in our house in Hampshire. My brother and sister-in-law came to stay one weekend and we took the children to the local zoo. Tim stayed at home to watch the cricket on the television. The telephone rang. It was Keith Percy asking to talk to me urgently.

'Nicola's taken the kids to the zoo. Can she ring you when she gets back, Keith.'

'Can you ask her to ring me in the office.' It is extremely unusual for fund managers to work in the office at weekends and I was very puzzled when I saw the message. I rang and got through to someone whose voice I did not recognize. He said that he would locate Keith for me. When he came to the telephone, I could hear that Keith was exhausted. He had been up all night. He explained that some irregularities had come to light in the European unit trusts and that the manager, Peter Young, had been suspended. It was likely that dealing in the funds would have to be stopped for a while until the matter was resolved. The Deutsche Bank, which had owned Morgan Grenfell since 1989, was prepared to buy out some of the unsuitable investments that had been made by Peter Young on behalf of the fund and the unit holders would have to be compensated for any loss. None of this directly affected my business. Keith was telling me because I was a member of the management committee.

I was stunned by what I heard. I could not comprehend how this could have happened. Our business was well controlled and all the fund managers' activities were carefully monitored. It was clear that I was going to have to return to London immediately and help Keith and my senior colleagues as much as I could. If dealings in the funds were stopped, there would be speculation in the newspapers about the whole matter and the UK pension fund clients would get nervous and need reassurance. If I was going back to London, it would be easier if all the children came and so we returned en masse.

In the event, there was little to do in those first days after Peter Young's activities were uncovered. We prepared and sent a letter to clients and I went to see the major consultants, but few clients wanted to see us in person. As more details came out in the press of what Peter Young had done, clients became concerned and I had to go and explain the situation to an ever increasing number of them. Peter Young had not had anything to do with the UK pension fund business and our pension funds were not invested in any of the funds that he managed, so there was no direct impact on them. However, naturally the clients were concerned that such a thing could have happened in the organization that was responsible for their pension funds. My maternity leave was cut short, but I did return home at regular intervals to feed the baby. I did not see why she should suffer as a result of Peter Young.

An internal inquiry was set up to look into what had

happened and whether anyone was responsible for any lapses in controlling Young over the period of time that he had been managing the European unit trusts. At first I thought it inconceivable that Keith's job would be at risk, but as time went on, I began to get vibes that it might be. I was horrified at the prospect of him being removed. He was a very meticulous man and totally honourable. If he had had any inkling of what was going on, he would have stopped it immediately.

I went to see a number of senior executives at Deutsche Morgan Grenfell to argue the case for keeping Keith. I stressed how important he was to my business and how difficult it would be for me to explain his removal to clients who knew him to be totally honest and trustworthy. I thought I was making progress in persuading those in authority that this would be a wrong move and so I was totally surprised when Keith was sacked together with four other senior executives in mid-October.

Telling the clients what had happened was the worst thing that I have ever had to do in my professional life. I am sure that they could tell that I did not agree with the decision, but I had to stick to the party line. I would go home at night and cry. I felt that the whole thing was very unfair. What was so sad was that our performance continued to be the best amongst the major houses in London. If it had not been for Peter Young, we would have been looking forward to our best year ever in terms of new business in the UK pension fund business and Keith would have been there with me, leading the team from the front.

Keith Percy and I had spent five years rebuilding Morgan

Grenfell's UK pension fund business together. They had been five exciting years. We had both taken a big career risk going there in the first place, but it had paid off and the industry was full of praise for what we had achieved. Keith was replaced with someone from within the bank who had a limited knowledge of my business. I knew that nothing would ever be the same again.

Morgan Grenfell Asset Management had lost a number of key executives and it was important to try to get a grip on the business as quickly as possible for the sake of the clients and the staff. Keith's successor, Robert Smith, had previously been responsible for running the development capital division for the bank. He was a Scottish accountant with a good professional track record. I knew him reasonably well and we had always got on. I had not wanted Keith to go but, given that he had, I was happy that Robert was taking over.

Robert had a difficult task ahead of him and I was determined to help him as much as I could. I wrote a note to him at the outset describing the business and highlighting the issues that needed to be addressed quickly. He appointed some management consultants to go through the systems and controls and I spent a great deal of time explaining to them how the business worked. Some of those lower down the organization began to express concern about whether Robert was the right person for the job and I told them I thought that he was.

Our new-business flow dried up almost completely in the UK pension fund business and we all found this frustrating. We knew that the scandal had been isolated from us, but there seemed to be an assumption amongst outsiders that if the controls in another part of our business had failed, the same could happen to us. We knew that this was not true and we produced a comprehensive report detailing exactly how our controls worked. Our existing clients found comfort in this, but it was clear that a period of time needed to elapse before we would start winning new business again. I knew that, as long as the performance held up, this would happen eventually.

The contrast between the mood of the organization during the summer and now, as we approached Christmas, was significant. We had gone from the fastest-growing pension fund business in London to a business reeling from the effects of the scandal. Morale was low and it was difficult to know what the future would hold.

ten

As I stood outside the front door of Morgan Grenfell on the Tuesday morning that I was suspended, I could not really comprehend what had happened to me. I had given everything to that company. When Georgie had been seriously ill, I had gone into the office because I did not want to let anyone down. I had returned early from maternity leave to help deal with the aftermath of the Peter Young affair. Now I was standing alone on the doorstep. I walked very slowly towards the taxis in front of Liverpool Street Station. Tim knew an employment lawyer and I had met her once before. I had no telephone to ring and forewarn her and so I just jumped in the cab and headed for her office.

The lawyer whom I was hoping to see was not there, but the senior partner agreed to see me. I felt very calm and shook him warmly by the hand, thanking him for seeing me at such short notice. I explained what had happened and he said that he could not really do anything until he had my contract of employment, my staff handbook and the letter detailing the allegations against me. I said that I did not know where my contract of employment or my staff handbook was and so I rang up Martyn Drain, the personnel director at Morgan Grenfell, and asked him to send copies of these to the solicitor. I then went to the stock exchange car park, got in my car and drove home.

As I walked up the steps to my house, I began to think about what I should say to Joan and the children. I took the view that I had to tell them exactly what had happened. Joan looked shocked, but she said that I should not worry as I was bound to get another job quickly and anyway I had looked very unhappy since Keith Percy had been sacked. I sat down on the sofa in the playroom and cooed at Antonia, who was now seven months old.

The telephone rang; it was an old school friend of mine ringing to say how sorry she was to hear about my suspension. How could she have known so quickly? I had only told the lawyer and Joan. She told me that the news had appeared on Reuters. She worked in the City and had a Reuters terminal on her desk. I was absolutely horrified. I had been told that I would get the chance to put my side of the story on Friday. How could I be re-instated if the whole world knew that I had been suspended and it had appeared on Reuters? After that, the telephone did not stop ringing. We have two lines and each time I took a call, the other one would start. Poor Joan would have to run up to my desk on the half-landing to answer it. Then the door-bell started ringing incessantly. Journalists and photographers were assembling outside. When Joan told them to go away and said, on my instructions, that I was unable to comment, they wrote notes and posted them through the front door.

They made it clear that they were not going away until they had got either a photograph or a statement.

The children looked rather bemused. Georgie put her arms round me and told me not to worry. I had drawn the curtains in the dining room so that the journalists could not see in, but every time the doorbell rang, Serena and Alice would peep through the curtains to try to see who it was. Georgie understood the gravity of the situation, but the others just thought that it was an exciting drama.

I went upstairs into the sitting room and sat down for a moment to contemplate what had just happened. Five hours ago I had been making a new business presentation to a local authority. I had been hauled out of the presentation and suspended from my job. I had been told not to speak to the press. The entire world now knew that I had been suspended because it had appeared on Reuters. Half the press corps was camped on my doorstep and the other half was on its way. I pinched myself very hard. Unfortunately, it was not a dream. This was reality. I still did not cry. I was past that. I had not even told Tim about my suspension as I had been busy talking to the lawyer. One of his colleagues had warned him that there was a rumour in the market that I had been suspended just before it appeared on Reuters.

'Don't be ridiculous,' he said, 'she was promoted last week.' When he read it on the screen, he was astounded. I had not spoken to my parents either. My grandmother read about it in the *Evening Standard* and phoned to tell them. The fact that my family had found out from the media rather than me made the situation seem even worse.

For once, Tim came home at a reasonable time. He put his arms around me and gave me a big hug. I recounted what had happened moment by moment and he was outraged. He knew exactly what had happened the previous week and we had talked endlessly about all the issues confronting Morgan Grenfell after the Peter Young affair. He knew that I had accepted the promotion I had been offered the previous Friday in good faith and that I was really looking forward to the new responsibilities it gave me.

'You've got to fight this. It's completely unfair.'

'I know it's unfair,' I replied. 'I've never been in this position before. I don't really know how to handle it.'

'What you need is a good lawyer.'

I spent that evening speaking to my sister-in-law, who is a solicitor, about whom I should ask to represent me. I had no particular attachment to the lawyer that I had seen when I had left Morgan Grenfell's offices; I just wanted the best. She suggested John Farr at Herbert Smith and Tim said that he had heard that he was excellent. The next morning I could hear the chatter of the reporters outside the front door when I awoke. Joan and Tim had told them that I was not allowed to speak to them, but reporters never take no for an answer. I spoke to John Farr, who agreed to represent me and suggested that we meet at once. I ran out of the front door, coat and handbag in hand, ignoring the cries of the reporters for comments. The photographers surrounded me as I jumped into the taxi, taking endless shots.

Every paper carried something about my suspension that day. There were quotes from the Morgan Grenfell press officer and comments about disloyalty and how I had been about to take a team to ABN Amro. I was shaking with anger as I read this. I had not been about to leave Morgan Grenfell. The newspapers insisted on calling me 'Super-woman' and claimed that this was the nickname that my team had given me. This was not true – their nickname for me was Brenda (*Private Eye*'s nickname for the Queen). The headlines all conveyed similar messages – Superwoman had fallen to Earth. We used to joke in the office about the fact that the newspapers seemed incapable of writing about me without referring to my children. Robert Smith said to me once, 'Why don't they ever refer to me as a father of two children?' There was no doubt in my mind that if I had not been a mother of five children, one of whom had leukaemia, I would not have been the subject of such intense interest. What annoyed me most, however, was that Morgan Grenfell's clumsy handling of the situation had made things worse.

Three days went by and the story continued to fill the financial pages of the newspapers with the odd comment in the women's pages. John Farr and I read them very carefully and he underlined the things that appeared to be common to all. Because I was still an employee of Morgan Grenfell and I had promised that I would not talk to the press, I was unable to refute the allegations that were being made against me. It seemed ridiculous that the newspapers continued to write about the story when there was nothing new to say.

Martyn Drain had said that there would be a good chance that I would be reinstated if I went to the disciplinary hearing on Friday, but I found it difficult to see how this could happen after the press had commented so extensively. On Thursday, I learned that Morgan Grenfell had arranged a press conference for 10 a.m. on Friday, two hours after the disciplinary hearing was due to start.

Why had they left it until Friday to have the disciplinary hearing? Could it have something to do with catching the Sunday press? I was convinced that Deutsche Morgan Grenfell's behaviour had been influenced more by their PR agency than by their lawyers. I could not see how I could possibly be given a fair hearing given all that had happened and it seemed to me that this was a clear case of constructive dismissal. John Farr agreed and he wrote to Fox Williams, Morgan Grenfell's lawyers, that day to say that the behaviour of their clients had been a clear repudiation of my contract and that I had been constructively dismissed. His letter went on to say that, in view of this, I would not be attending the disciplinary hearing. Later I would have to decide to pursue a claim through the courts.

Finally, I was in a position to say something to the press and publicly to refute the allegations that had been made against me. That evening, I gave an interview to the *Financial Times* in an attempt to set the record straight. What most concerned me was that my clients would think that I had been trying to take a team of people to ABN Amro and that we had been about to desert them. I wanted them to know that I had accepted the new job offered to me by Robert Smith in good faith and that I had intended to do it to the best of my abilities. I wanted them to know that I had been motivated by a passionate desire to keep my team together because I believed that it was the best institutional team in the City and by a determination that the rest of Morgan Grenfell, which in recent months had proved so badly lacking, should share the same values and philosophy as the UK business.

I left the lawyers' offices at about 8.30 p.m. It was a desperately cold evening and there was not a free taxi in sight. As I walked past Liverpool Street Station and the offices of Morgan Grenfell, I found it difficult to believe that I was no longer an employee and that I would not be going to that building each day. I reached London Wall and still there were no taxis. I walked down Moorgate and past the Mansion House and then decided that I would go home on the tube. There had been large photographs of me in the *Evening Standard* every day since I had been suspended and I could feel the gaze of half the carriage on me as I sat down. I got as far as Victoria where I took a taxi for the rest of the journey. I could not stand being stared at any longer.

When I finally arrived at our house, there was still a large number of journalists outside my door and photographers were lying in wait. The minute that I climbed out of the taxi, they appeared from nowhere. I ran into the door and closed it with a sigh of relief. I drew all the curtains at the front of the house and hoped that they would go home to bed and leave me alone. I could not eat anything and I certainly did not feel like watching television.

I rang Frances Davies, one of my closest friends and a colleague at Morgan Grenfell, to get her thoughts on what I should do next. We talked for about two hours that evening.

'I think you would regret it if you started pursuing this through the courts,' she said. 'It wouldn't be good for you and it wouldn't be good for the family. You'll get another job and you will continue to be successful. Whether it was right or wrong, I think you should accept what's happened and move on.'

'I know you're right that it wouldn't do me any good to go to court, but it isn't fair and why should I let Morgan Grenfell get away with it?'

'Look, Nicola. You know you haven't been happy since Keith left.'

'That doesn't mean that I wanted to leave too. I've got a baby and a sick child. I just can't imagine what it's going to be like walking into a new organization where I've got to start all over again with the pressures that I've had on me. I liked the people I was working with at Morgan Grenfell. I'm going to miss my team.'

'You're very strong. You'll cope.'

Eventually, I went to bed. I lay awake thinking about what I was going to do for some hours. I really had meant what I said to Frances. I wanted to work with my team; I did not want to have to start all over again. I had had an extremely difficult two years with Georgie's illness and the Peter Young affair and I really was weary of it all. I have always been a very strong person emotionally, but I was finding the situation very hard to deal with. I finally went to sleep at about 3 a.m., but was awoken by voices outside the house at about 6 a.m. Having read all about my side of the story in the *Financial Times*, every other newspaper wanted to talk to me and Sky News had appeared as well.

I rubbed my eyes and felt a great sense of irritation at being woken after so little sleep. I rolled over and tried to go back to sleep, but their chattering continued. I got up, retrieved the baby from her cot and got dressed. Tim kissed me goodbye as he was leaving for work. He pushed his way through the waiting journalists, warning the photographers not to photograph him and the majority respected his wishes.

John Farr and I were supposed to have been at the disciplinary hearing, but as we had told Morgan Grenfell that I was not attending, we had agreed that I would spend the day at home and we would meet again on Monday to discuss what I should do next. I ran down the stairs when the children had left for school, babe in arms, and opened the door and spoke to the assembled crowd.

'Rather than annoying me by standing on my doorstep, it's about time that you lot helped me. I am going to give the baby her breakfast and then you are coming with me to Morgan Grenfell's offices to see if we can get my job back.' There were gleeful smiles from the audience and ripples of laughter as I closed the door.

Minutes later, Antonia having had her breakfast, I grabbed my handbag and the car keys and told the entourage to meet me at the bandstand in Finsbury Circus. I climbed into Tim's red Alfa Romeo sports car and sped off. One of the photographers gave a lift to a couple of the others and insisted on following me. I stared straight ahead, determined that I was going to try and get reinstated. I knew it was unlikely that I would achieve my aim, but I did not think that it could do any harm if I tried.

Standing on top of the bandstand in Finsbury Circus, I looked towards the offices of Morgan Grenfell Asset Management and took a deep breath. It was a cold, bright day and I was not wearing a coat, but I felt hot. When everyone was present, I turned to them and said, 'We are going to go into the building, walk past the security guard and go up to the third floor to Robert Smith's office. Follow me.' We marched across Finsbury Circus. One of the journalists asked if I was scared and I replied, 'Not at all. I'm just hoping that it doesn't get nasty when we try to get in. I'm sure we won't succeed.'

But we did. The security guard was sitting behind the desk when we walked in and took a minute to realize what was happening. When he saw the six journalists and photographers behind me, he rose to his feet and began to come towards me. I pointed at him and said, 'You lay one finger on me and I'm calling the police and you lay one finger on them and I will do the same.' He shrank back and let us pass and I walked up the stairs with my band of supporters.

We got to the third floor and I opened the doors and entered the open-plan floor where I used to work. One of my senior colleagues, Patrick Disney, was standing in front of me and looked as though he had seen a ghost. There was general panic and shouting as members of my team realized what was happening. I could not see any of my close associates; Adrian Frost and Charlie Curtis were not at their desks and I did not see Frances either. I took no notice of the attempts of those who were there to stop me and marched through the middle of the room towards Robert's office, photographers and journalists still in tow. It was a bit of an anti-climax when I arrived in his office and he was not there.

For some reason, Martyn Drain, the personnel director, Robert's secretary and a marketing person from the international team were in there. There was a struggle as Martyn and some of the fund managers together with some security guards tried to eject the journalists and photographers. Eventually, they succeeded and I found myself in the room with the three who had been there on my arrival. We looked at each other awkwardly and Martyn said something about me not being allowed on the premises.

'Where is Robert? I want to see him,' I said and his secretary replied that he was out. 'Thank you,' I said and opened the door and walked back through the office. Some people smiled at me, others looked completely shocked by the whole event. 'Justice will be done,' I said loudly and left the room. It sounded melodramatic, but I meant it. What had happened to me was unfair and I was trying to do something about it.

I found myself back on the pavement with the journalists and photographers and we laughed and laughed. I have to say that I felt a hundred times better after having done that.

Having failed to see Robert Smith, I decided that the next port of call should be 6 Bishopsgate where Michael

Dobson, Chairman of Morgan Grenfell Asset Management and Chief Executive of Deutsche Morgan Grenfell, had his office. By the time we arrived there, word had spread about the happenings at 20 Finsbury Circus and Norman Marks (ex-vice squad), who was head of security for the group, was standing next to the receptionist at the front desk. I politely asked to see Michael Dobson. The receptionist had some difficulty in getting through to his secretary, but eventually did so. She said I should sit in the foyer and she would let me know in due course if he would be able to see me.

By this time, the posse of journalists and photographers had grown to about fifteen and so we all sat down and talked about what had happened to me, the history of the case and what I could do about my plight. They were all extremely sympathetic and I told them that, as I did not believe that I would get a fair hearing in London, I would have to go to Frankfurt if Michael Dobson refused to see me. We waited for twenty minutes and then the receptionist politely told me that Michael Dobson would not be able to see me. One of the journalists told me when the next flight to Frankfurt was and which terminal to go to.

By going to Germany that day, I inadvertently propelled the story on to the front pages of all the national newspapers. I did not go, as some have accused, in order to gain more publicity. I went because I genuinely believed that I was more likely to get a fair hearing there. I did try to get my superiors in London to talk to me before I took the step of travelling to Frankfurt, but they would not do so.

When I decided that I had no option but to go, I rang John Farr and told him what I was doing. He said that he would ring the Deutsche Bank in Frankfurt and arrange for someone to see me. He felt that this would be better than me arriving without having made any formal contact. I agreed to ring him on my arrival in Germany.

By the time I got to Heathrow, a crowd of journalists, photographers and television cameras was waiting for me. A Reuters reporter had been with me earlier in the City and had carried the story that I was on my way to Frankfurt. I had only a few minutes to buy my ticket and check in, but as I walked towards the Lufthansa sales desk, I was engulfed by the crowd of notebook-carrying journalists and a television camera was thrust in my face. I had to say something, so I just said that I had been unfairly treated, no one would listen to me in London, so I was going to Frankfurt. I pushed my way through them and went to the ticket desk. Those who were intending to follow me had bought their tickets moments before.

Other passengers looked on in amazement, wondering what was going on. Who was this woman who was causing such a huge amount of press interest? As I paid for my ticket and checked in, the cameras were constantly flashing. The plane was due to take off in fifteen minutes and I had to walk extremely fast to the gate with the journalists and photographers in hot pursuit. Some of them were joining me on the plane, others were staying behind, but they all accompanied me right to the door of the plane. It did not seem to matter that some of them did not have boarding passes. The flight attendants looked as bemused as the passengers.

I sat in my seat and fastened my seat belt with a sigh. What a morning! Tim did not know anything about the events so far and I was sure that he was going to be pretty cross when he found out. I knew that his instinct would have been to let the lawyers handle it. On the other hand, I knew that he shared my feelings of injustice and that he would agree that it was right that I should seek a fair hearing. I had tried to ring him on my way to Heathrow, but he had been in a meeting.

I thought I would have time to reflect on the plane and work out what I was going to say when I arrived at Deutsche Bank's offices, but soon I was surrounded by journalists again. ITN on one side, the *Telegraph* on the other, *The Times* and the *Mail* in front of me. The photographers sat together near the back of the plane, having a rest after the mad rush to catch it. A couple of them had been with me since the beginning of the day, but the majority had joined me at the airport.

'Why is it that you are all women?' I asked the journalists.

'Because it's a girlie story,' one of them replied.

'I've never seen any of you before,' I said. 'You aren't financial journalists are you?'

'No,' they replied, 'we're from the news desks.' That was my first indication that the story was about to be projected on to a different level entirely.

When we landed in Frankfurt, we walked towards the exit and were greeted by a barrage of more journalists, photographers and television cameras. There seemed to be even more at that end than there had been in London. Crowds of people gathered to watch the spectacle. They clearly had no idea who I was or what I was doing in Frankfurt airport but curiosity had got the better of them.

I got my mobile phone out and telephoned John Farr to see if he had managed to arrange for me to meet with anyone from the Deutsche Bank, but I was told that no one would see me. I was bitterly disappointed. But I did not feel that I could turn back without trying to get a meeting, so I got into a taxi and drove to the famous twin towers that house the Deutsche Bank's headquarters and dominate the Frankfurt skyline.

There was snow on the ground. It was pretty cold and I had left home that morning without a coat, but somehow I was oblivious to the temperature. The adrenalin was keeping me going. When I arrived at Deutsche Bank's offices, I was greeted by a man who said, 'Mrs Horlick, we have been expecting you. Please come this way.' I was suspicious and asked whom I was going to see. I imagined that there were one or two people who were feeling pretty annoyed with me in that building and might wish to express this. It had seemed courageous to come to Frankfurt and confront my ultimate employers, but now I was here, I was scared. The man shrugged his shoulders and said that he had just been told to take me to a meeting room. I turned to the thirty journalists and asked if anyone was prepared to come into the meeting with me to act as a witness. One of the representatives from Reuters in Frankfurt agreed to do so.

A few minutes later, we were sitting in a meeting room

high up in one of the towers. Two men came into the room. One was a senior member of the legal department and the other was an equally senior member of the human resources department. They shook our hands and were extremely courteous. They asked me to recount the events of the last few days, which I did. At the end, the lawyer, Dr Bosch, said that it sounded as though there had been a number of misunderstandings. I thought that this was a rather charitable interpretation, but I nodded my head.

'What do you want?' he asked.

'Reinstatement,' I said. 'I enjoy my job and I like working with my team.'

'And if this is not possible?'

'Compensation,' I said. He nodded and said that he could not make any judgements without first finding out what the other side of the story was. He promised that he would do this. At the end of the conversation, he asked the girl from Reuters how long we had known each other and she said that we had just met outside the building. I had said at the beginning of the meeting that she was from Reuters and that I had brought her as an independent witness, but he had not properly understood.

I think Dr Bosch was a little horrified when he realized that a journalist had just listened to our entire conversation, but she assured him that she was there in a personal capacity and would not repeat anything that she had heard to anyone. However, we agreed that in her professional capacity, it would be helpful if she could put a statement out on the wires and she and Dr Bosch then decided on a form of words. The gist of the statement was that we had had a full and frank discussion and that the Deutsche Bank would be investigating the matter further.

Dr Bosch arranged for a car to take us to the airport and we were taken to an underground garage. The girl from Reuters actually lived in Frankfurt, but she said that she would come with me and talk over what had been said if it would help. We went to the furthest reaches of the airport after I had checked in to avoid the journalists.

'They'll be standing outside waiting for us,' she said. 'I'd better tell them that we've gone. They'll be freezing!' She rang one of her colleagues who had been outside with her when we had disappeared to our meeting. In fact they had been allowed to wait in the lobby which was civilized of the Deutsche Bank.

About forty minutes after she had called, ITN found us in the café and came up to us, cameras rolling, to ask what had been the outcome of the meeting. I was taken by surprise and my mind went completely blank, so I had to ask the girl from Reuters to tell me what the agreed statement was. A minute later, her mobile telephone rang and her office told her that Morgan Grenfell had put out a statement saying that the Germans had only seen me out of courtesy and London was still dealing with the matter. I was very irritated by this. At that stage, however, I still believed that Dr Bosch would stand by his word and look into the matter.

By the time I got on the plane, I was completely exhausted. The same women who had been with me on the way out reassembled on the plane. They were eager to know how it had gone and I told them. They all thought it sounded hopeful. I gave two of them a lift back to central London. It should have been the end of a pretty extraordinary day, but when I returned home, the City Editor of one of the Sunday newspapers was waiting. I had been advised that I should give them an interview, but I had forgotten all about it.

I found it very difficult to give a dispassionate view of all that had happened. During the interview, I was frequently close to tears. By the time we had finished, it was 1.30 a.m. As I closed the front door, I could not help thinking that I was closing the door on a chapter of my life. Morgan Grenfell would not give me my job back. There would be too much loss of face. It was desperately unfair, but life was unfair. I knew deep down that I was going to have to come to terms with it and get on with my life.

As I had expected, Tim did not think that going to Frankfurt had been the right thing to do. We sat down and I explained what had happened and how Dr Bosch had listened to what I had to say.

'He won't be allowed to do anything. London won't let him interfere.'

'Deutsche Bank owns Morgan Grenfell. If they think that the thing has been badly handled, they may well intervene.'

'I don't think that's very likely, but maybe you're right.'

The next day, every newspaper carried the story on its front page. The journalists and photographers were outside again. We had no food and I needed to go shopping. I could not bear the thought of being followed all day by an entourage. As lunch-time approached, I could wait no longer, so I opened the door and negotiated with the crowd that if I went to the park and let them photograph me and the children, they would leave us alone for the rest of the day. To give them their due, they stuck to this. A couple of days later, a snide article appeared in one of the papers saying that it was stretching the imagination to think that I had just been strolling through the park with the children and the photographers just happened to be there. Quite clearly, it was pre-arranged, but I needed some privacy and that was the only way to get rid of them.

On Sunday morning, there were yet more journalists and a television crew outside the house. I do not know what they could possibly think had changed over the previous twenty-four hours. It was the weekend after all. I spoke to my brother and we agreed that the children and I would spend the day with him and his family in Primrose Hill. I needed to escape. I felt like a prisoner in my own home.

As I put down the telephone, tears came into my eyes. I could not stand much more of this. I rang Frances and asked her if she could arrange a meeting between me and Robert Smith so that we could sort out what the facts actually were once and for all. She said she would try.

Later that morning, she rang back and said she had tried really hard, but Robert Smith was very concerned that the press would get to hear about it. I said that if we both agreed not to tell the press, then why should they find out.

Was it not more important that the truth came out? There seemed to be nothing I could do to get justice. I sat on my bed sobbing.

The time came to load the children into the car to go to my brother's house. The television crew, who were from BBC 2's *Money Programme*, followed me down the road to the car asking me questions and then filmed me strapping the baby into the car. I reiterated that I had not done anything wrong in my view and that I wanted my job back. I begged them all to go away and not to follow me to my brother's house. They gave assurances that they would not and they did not.

Herbert Smith had suggested that I should take advice from a public relations consultant which I did. He advised me not to say anything to the press thereafter. There had been so much coverage that no one could be in any doubt what my side of the story was. I spent much of the next week at Herbert Smith's offices with John Farr. We wrote to Dr Bosch and asked him to confirm that he was pursuing the matter. I was extremely disappointed when he wrote and said that he was not going to be involved any further and that London was dealing with the matter. He had clearly been stamped on from on high.

Meanwhile, Morgan Grenfell's lawyers were busy collecting statements from my ex-colleagues. They were said to be incriminating. Since they all knew perfectly well that I had accepted the job offered to me by Robert Smith in good faith and was not leaving, I could not understand how this could be. There were allegations that I had been trying to demoralize my team by telling them that their bonuses would be cut by 30 per cent. This was completely untrue. On 6 January, eight days before I was suspended, I had been asked by one member of the team what his bonus would be. I knew that he had been concerned that bonuses would be cut as a result of the Peter Young affair and so I sought to reassure him by telling him that his bonus would be 65 per cent higher than in 1996. This was the result of my lobbying in the run up to Christmas. How could anyone construe this as trying to demoralize someone?

I was greatly saddened when I heard via my solicitor what my former colleagues had been saying. I had worked with these people for almost six years. I regarded them as my friends and I thought that we respected each other. Why were they trying to make out that I had done and said things that I had not? They had clearly decided that I was gone for ever and they wanted to put themselves in the best possible light. In addition, their bonuses were due and, of course, there was my bonus to be shared out. It was understandable, but very difficult to come to terms with. I felt very alone, very vulnerable and sapped of all my usual strength.

I had had a great deal of luck during my career. I suppose it was inevitable that eventually something would go wrong, but who could have envisaged that it would go quite so spectacularly wrong. All the letters I received implored me to keep on fighting. I felt like I had been shipwrecked and was about to be overcome by an enormous wave. I could not see how I was going to rebuild my life in the light of what had happened.

'You have got to pull yourself together, my dear,' a kind friend told me a few weeks later. He was a client of mine and I had turned to him in despair for advice. We had agreed to meet at the Reform Club. We sat on green leather chairs in the library. There were only two other people in the room, both elderly men reading newspapers. This was just as well as I burst into tears halfway into the sorry tale.

'You have the strength to deal with this,' said my wise companion.

'It's all too much for me,' I said, weeping. He handed me a beautifully ironed handkerchief. 'It's the accumulation of Georgie's illness, Keith being sacked and now this. I've tried to be brave. Maybe I've been too brave and now I can't cope.'

'Nonsense,' he said, 'of course you can.'

This was a turning point. The outpouring of all my anxiety in the rather unlikely surroundings of the Reform Club library made me feel better. As my kind friend later wrote to me in a letter, it was probably a first for the club to have an hysterical woman in its library, but the other occupants did not seem too concerned about it.

Some months have now passed since I left Morgan Grenfell, but complete strangers are still coming up to me in the street and asking me if I am Nicola Horlick. Every taxi driver in London seems to know who I am. Shortly after the storm over my departure from Morgan Grenfell, I walked towards a taxi in Piccadilly and the driver pulled down the window and said, 'London or Frankfurt?' I thought that was rather witty.

It is disconcerting when you are no longer another anonymous face among the crowd. It is so much easier to go about your business when no one knows who you are and it is off-putting when, wherever you are, people stare at you or start whispering to a companion who then turns their head to confirm whether the identification is correct. At first it made me feel awkward and embarrassed, but I have learned to cope with it now.

In some ways it is comforting to know that people are supportive. Those who have come up and spoken to me have been universally so. The majority are women, but some men have voiced support as well. I was recently standing with the children in a queue to get into the Hard Rock Café at Universal Pictures in Florida and a man came up to me and said, 'Are you who I think you are?'

'Sorry?' I replied, hoping that he would think that he was mistaken and go away.

'Are you who I think you are?' he asked again and it was clear that he was not going to go away until I confirmed that I was indeed who he thought I was.

'Yes,' I said weakly.

'I think you're wonderful,' he said. 'Keep on fighting.' There are days when I feel on top of the world and days when I want to curl up and die. I was in a melancholy mood that day and the intervention of this man when I least expected it cheered me up for the rest of the day.

I also received a large amount of correspondence from members of the public who felt for me in the ghastly situation I found myself in. Only one letter was critical. It was from a lady pensioner who said that I should shut up and accept that I was very lucky to have a wonderful husband and five lovely children and did I realize how much she had to live on each week? I think she was slightly missing the point. It was not the money I minded about. It was the injustice.

I have learned a great deal about other human beings. I now realize that you can never be true friends with work colleagues. When it comes to a conflict, they are likely to look after themselves and I now realize that I cannot blame them for that. I am not the first person to lose my job. It happens to thousands of people every week. My removal from Morgan Grenfell hurt my pride, but I am lucky that I quickly had the opportunity to start again. I am now working for a French bank who were willing to look beyond all the publicity and to judge me on what I have achieved professionally.

I look forward with optimism. I have come through some difficult times and I know now that I can cope with anything. The constant support of my family stopped me from sinking without trace. They helped me to pull myself together and my self-confidence has returned. My work is stimulating and it is even possible that I may end up happier in the long run. Life is difficult, and no one ever goes up in a straight line.

Losing my job was not the worst thing that has ever happened to me. Being told that Georgie had leukaemia was worse. Finding out that she had relapsed was worse. Nearly losing her was worse. Having a sick child has put life into perspective for me. I would not care if I had no money and no material possessions if I could have Georgie's health. Before she got ill, I thought I could have it all. After all we've been through, I've learned that no one can. Once you know what's really important, having that is enough. The most important thing to me is that Georgie should stay well.

epilogue

SUNDAY 29 JUNE 1997

Yesterday, my father died. It was unexpected and I still cannot believe that it has really happened. Last year, he had an operation to replace a valve in his heart. We were told that there was a 98 per cent success rate and he made an excellent recovery. He was fit and carried no extra weight and there was every reason to believe that he would live for many years. At the beginning of last week, he came out in a red rash, developed a fever and became delirious. My mother called an ambulance and he was taken to the hospital in Chichester. It soon became apparent that it was an infection around the base of the new valve and my mother was told that it was most unlucky that this had happened, especially so long after the operation.

On Wednesday, he was transferred to Southampton and an echo was done to check whether the valve was working. It was not and so he had an emergency operation to replace it. We were told that he was making an excellent recovery and he only spent one day in intensive care, one more in intermediate care and then was moved to an open cardiac ward. On Friday evening, I spoke to him for half an hour on the telephone. He sounded slightly dopey because of the morphine, but we had a normal conversation. I was surprised at how well he sounded considering what he had just been through. On Saturday morning, my mother spent several hours with him and the nurse told her what wonderful progress he had made and how pleased the doctors were.

Later that afternoon while he was asleep, the nurse went to check his temperature. He was dead. His heart had stopped. I was on my way to the hospital from London and rang my mother when I was just coming into Southampton to check which ward he was in. A friend answered the telephone and told me that my father was dead. I had Georgie, Alice and Serena in the car. I put the telephone down.

'Grandpa is dead, darlings.' I began to sob. 'Grandpa is dead.'

Somehow I managed to drive down the M27 to Chichester. Tears were streaming down my face and I could barely see where I was going. I had to get to my mother. The children were howling and the car was like a ball of emotion rolling ever nearer to my parents' house.

My mother was in the garden. She was walking round and round, trying to come to terms with what had happened. I jumped out of the car and ran to her, clasping her in my arms. The children followed me and the five of us stood huddled together, united in our grief. My brother had been on the way to the hospital too and had arrived to be told the news. He saw my father's body and then came home.

'Come with me to the hospital now. You've got to come and say goodbye to Father,' he said to me.

'I can't.'

'It'll make you feel better, I promise you. Come with me.'

My mother and I did go and my brother was right. It did make me feel better. I did not want to see my father's body because I was worried that he would have an expression of pain and anguish. I wanted to remember him as his normal smiling self. When I saw him, he looked as though he was asleep, totally serene and at peace. I was not frightened. I touched his head. He was cold, but not that cold. I kissed him.

My father had had the greatest influence on me. He was highly intelligent, but would always say that we were all cleverer than him. He was modest almost to the point of being irritating. He was wise. He was affectionate. He always gave me his total support and he never criticized me.

When I was Georgie's age, I used to sit at my desk in my bedroom and do my homework. When it got to six o'clock, I would start to listen for the front door. My father took the same train every night and always arrived home at the same time. The moment I heard the door go, I would run downstairs and hug him. When I went to Cheltenham, I could not do that any more and I hated it. He was not cross with me when I ran away. He knew I missed him and my mother and he did not think I should be reprimanded for that.

When I worked with him at Roy Wilson, Dickson, I loved being with him and learned a great deal from him. It struck me that the staff who worked for him adored him. He never demanded anything from them, but always asked them politely to do things for him. If they had a problem, he would talk to them and help as much as he could. They gave him their total loyalty in return. He had great business acumen, but he never talked about his success. He gave the impression of having been lucky to have inherited a family business, but in fact his skill ensured that it became substantial enough to mean that we would all be well provided for financially.

The one great sadness in his life was that Georgie had been so ill. My parents spent hours and hours in the hospital with Georgie and me throughout both her illnesses. My father gave her love and encouragement and he even stayed overnight in the hospital with her occasionally.

I still cannot believe that I will never see my father again. He was only sixty-six. Too young to die. I will always love him. I will always miss him.

MY GRANDPA

Kind and gentle,
Generous and loving,

Living his life as an angel,
Liked by everyone who knew him.

Quiet and calm,
Thoughtful and caring,

Never being horrible to anyone or shouting at them.
Because he was all of these things, I loved him and still do.

Georgina Horlick
29 June 1997

All Pan Books are available at your local bookshop or newsagent, or can be ordered direct from the publisher. Indicate the number of copies required and fill in the form below.

Send to: Macmillan General Books C.S.
              Book Service By Post
              PO Box 29, Douglas I-O-M
              IM99 1BQ

or phone: 01624 675137, quoting title, author and credit card number.

or fax: 01624 670923, quoting title, author, and credit card number.

or Internet: http://www.bookpost.co.uk

Please enclose a remittance* to the value of the cover price plus 75 pence per book for post and packing. Overseas customers please allow £1.00 per copy for post and packing.

*Payment may be made in sterling by UK personal cheque, Eurocheque, postal order, sterling draft or international money order, made payable to Book Service By Post.

Alternatively by Access/Visa/MasterCard

Card No. ☐☐☐☐☐☐☐☐☐☐☐☐☐☐☐☐☐☐☐

Expiry Date ☐☐☐☐☐☐☐☐☐☐☐☐☐☐☐☐☐☐☐

Signature   _____

Applicable only in the UK and BFPO addresses.

While every effort is made to keep prices low, it is sometimes necessary to increase prices at short notice. Pan Books reserve the right to show on covers and charge new retail prices which may differ from those advertised in the text or elsewhere.

NAME AND ADDRESS IN BLOCK CAPITAL LETTERS PLEASE

Name _____

Address _____

_____

_____

_____

8/95

Please allow 28 days for delivery.
Please tick box if you do not wish to receive any additional information. ☐